Game Design Deep Dive

Game Design Critic Josh Bycer continues the *Deep Dive* series with an examination of cozy games. The market for coziness has grown dramatically, thanks to showcases like Wholesome Direct and consumers wanting something to help them relax in a stressful world.

Key Features:

- Discusses the success of *Stardew Valley* and how it became the poster child for cozy games, and offers a brief history of the genre.
- Examines UI/UX design and how to have effective playtesting done for your game, both required lessons for developers today.
- Looks at what it means to build a low-stakes game while still offering progression and rewards to keep people invested.

Joshua Bycer is a Game Design Analyst with over a decade of experience writing for major sites, creating content on YouTube, and authoring the *Game Design Deep Dive* series. In that time, through Game-Wisdom.com, he has interviewed hundreds of game developers and members of the industry about what it means to design video games.

Game Design Deep Dive

Cozy Games

Joshua Bycer

CRC Press is an imprint of the
Taylor & Francis Group, an **informa** business

Designed cover image: Peggy Shu and Kenneth Oum

First edition published 2027
by CRC Press
2385 NW Executive Center Drive, Suite 320, Boca Raton FL 33431

and by CRC Press
4 Park Square, Milton Park, Abingdon, Oxon, OX14 4RN

CRC Press is an imprint of Taylor & Francis Group, LLC

Library of Congress Cataloging-in-Publication Data
Names: Bycer, Joshua author
Title: Game design deep dive : cozy games / Joshua Bycer.
Other titles: Cozy games
Description: First edition. | Boca Raton, FL : CRC Press, 2026. |
Series: Game design deep dive | Includes bibliographical references and index.
Identifiers: LCCN 2025046536 (print) | LCCN 2025046537 (ebook) |
ISBN 9781041087779 hbk | ISBN 9781041087762 pbk | ISBN 9781003646860 ebk
Subjects: LCSH: Video games--Design | Video games--Psychological aspects |
Video games--Social aspects | User interfaces (Computer systems)
Classification: LCC GV1469.3 .B929 2026 (print) | LCC GV1469.3 (ebook) |
DDC 794.8--dc23/eng/20260526
LC record available at https://lccn.loc.gov/2025046536
LC ebook record available at https://lccn.loc.gov/2025046537

ISBN: 978-1-041-08777-9 (hbk)
ISBN: 978-1-041-08776-2 (pbk)
ISBN: 978-1-003-64686-0 (ebk)

DOI: 10.1201/9781003646860

Typeset in Minion
by SPi Technologies India Pvt Ltd (Straive)

Contents

Preface

In a way, I'm surprised that I'm writing this book on cozy games – coming from someone who frequently plays every game they can find at the highest difficulty, and I rarely have the time these days to unwind. Each book gets dedicated to at least one game, and this gave me the opportunity to go back and really get into *Stardew Valley* and see just how big it has gotten since I first played it in 2018.

While cozy games are meant to be relaxing and low stakes, I hope everyone pays attention to the chapter on UI/UX design, as that is often the first big stumbling block in building a game.

Additional Books

If you enjoyed this entry and want to learn more about design, you can read my other works:

20 Essential Games to Study – A high-level look at 20 unique games that are worth studying their design to be inspired by or for a historical look at the game industry.

Game Design Deep Dive: Platformers – The first entry in the *Game Design Deep Dive* series focusing on 2D and 3D platformer design. A top-to-bottom discussion of the history, mechanics, and design of the game industry's most recognizable and long-lasting genre.

Game Design Deep Dive: Roguelikes – For this *Deep Dive*, we're focusing on the rise and design of roguelike games. A look back at how the genre started, what makes the design unique, and an across-the-board discussion on how it has become the basis for new designs by modern developers.

Game Design Deep Dive: Horror – In this entry, it's about the philosophy and psychology behind horror. Looking at the history of the genre, I explored what it means to create a scary game or use horror elements in any genre.

Game Design Deep Dive: F2P – The mobile game and free-to-play markets are discussed in this *Deep Dive* to have a discussion about ethical and predatory practices in mobile games.

Game Design Deep Dive: Trading and Collectible Card Games – Collectible card games and the entire philosophy of deck building design are discussed, along with looking at how card manufacturers turn rarity into big bucks.

Game Design Deep Dive: Role Playing Games – This entry focuses on the role-playing game genre to look at the history of CRPG and JRPG design, and lessons on abstraction-based design.

Game Design Deep Dive: Real Time Strategy – Celebrating the history and design of real-time strategy games with a talk about the major names and why the genre fell out of mainstream favor in the 2010s.

Game Design Deep Dive: Soulslikes – The first entry to focus on a specific subgenre of design, this book tackles soulslike design as well as a discussion on difficulty in games.

Game Design Deep Dive: Shooters – A look at the history and design of shooters and reflex-driven gameplay and gunplay.

Game Design Deep Dive: Metroidvanias – For this entry, it's about one of the most confusing genres to understand from outside the industry. We talked about how it got started, how indies ran away with it, and the challenges of designing one, given how popular it is.

Acknowledgments

- Michael Berthaud
- Ben Bishop
- D.S
- Jason Ellis
- Jake Everitt
- Thorn Falconeye
- Puppy Games
- Mark Griffin
- Luke Hughes
- Adriaan Jansen
- Jonathan Ku
- Aron Linde
- Josh Mull
- Rey Obomsawin
- Janet Oblinger
- Onslaught
- David Pittman

Social Media

- Email: gamewisdombusiness@gmail.com
- My YouTube channel where I post daily design videos and developer interviews: youtube.com/c/game-wisdom.
- Main site: Game-Wisdom.com
- Twitter and BlueSky: GWBycer

Time to Dive Into Cozy Games

Cozy and Wholesome Games

1.1 Let's Get Cozy

Welcome to what may be the hardest book to write on one of the most relaxing types of games. Cozy games and the wholesome movement has been another gateway for people to get into games who aren't into the standard affair. And to that point, many indie developers have been making a name for themselves in this untapped market over the end of the 2010s to now (Figure 1.1).

The goal of this book is to explain what makes a game cozy, how it differs from casual games, and why despite the very low stakes of it, it is still a challenge to get right.

This will be the shortest design book in the *Deep Dive* Series, as "cozy" in and of itself is a thematic genre, and like horror, is not beholden to any one specific game **system** or style of gameplay. And to that point, it's why this book is going to focus on a critical component of game design.

DOI: 10.1201/9781003646860-1

Figure 1.1

Welcome to a new *Deep Dive* as we're getting cozy to talk about how a new generation of games is helping people relax.

1.2 Utilizing User Experience

Each *Deep Dive* has had a section specifically to discuss the user interface and the user experience of a game (**UI/UX**). For this book, instead of an advanced design chapter, which doesn't go with making a cozy game, I'm going to focus on UI/UX design and the best playtesting practices. While this is crucial for cozy and casual games, learning about UI/UX will make you a better designer, as these two points are often what separates bad games from good ones and good ones from award winners (Figure 1.2).

Whenever I examine games, the UI/UX is always on the front of my mind, because no matter how great your game is, if someone is frustrated or annoyed by your game from the first minute of turning it on, they are not going to stay with the game or continue following the studio.

And whether you are making the most relaxing or the most stress-inducing game, these are lessons you need to learn, and it's better to pick them up now rather than making a game and learning them the hard way by having your game fail on release. The best games are usually paired with a great UI/UX, and that can only come with effectively studying the genre in question and understanding how someone plays your game. Even though what this book is going to discuss doesn't cover every genre, the practices and procedures you'll learn are universal.

Figure 1.2

Every genre has its own standard practices for UI/UX, and the earlier you learn how to study and implement them will make you a better designer.

2

Cozy Theming

2.1 What Are Cozy Games?

If you're someone who only plays mainstream games and has never touched the indie market, you may not know what we're talking about. Cozy games began as an off-branch of casual games and are meant to be games that avoid challenging or stressful **mechanics**. Over the 2010s, cozy games have grown into their own style of game separate from casual games. These are games that are meant to be enjoyed by everyone and provide a way for someone to relax and unwind. In Chapter 5, I'll discuss more about the differences between casual and cozy game definitions, as there are substantial differences.

Most cozy games by their design are meant to be simplistic experiences, but more importantly, there is a specific vibe to cozy games that goes with the theme. The player is not supposed to be fighting for their lives against monsters, but instead it could be about petting cats, watering plants, running a BnB, and so on (Figure 2.1). As we'll talk about, combat can fit in a cozy game if it goes with the theme of the design.

Another part of cozy games that will come up throughout this book is "wholesome games." In a way, they are a niche of a niche whose definition is often debated

 DOI: 10.1201/9781003646860-2

Figure 2.1

Cozy games are meant to be relaxing and can be about easy to learn gameplay or focusing on an original story.

among fans and developers. Both styles are about the same goal – providing someone with a game that is meant to be relaxing and easy to get into. This takes us to an important concept and distinction that you need to grasp if you want to break into this market yourself.

2.2 Lowering the Stakes

Video games for more than 40 years now have often focused on high stakes – the player must save the world, defeat the evil one, run a company, and many more. High stakes often go with the power fantasy aspect of video games – the player is the only one who can save the world because of how amazing they are at everything they do.

Cozy and wholesome games tend to focus on low-stakes stories and gameplay (Figure 2.2). Instead of the fate of the world hanging in the balance, the worst thing that could happen is… nothing. A common debate for the longest time is: "What is a video game?", which extends from "What is a game?" A game by its definition must have a win and a loss state – someone must win, and someone must lose. As a player, you agree to an unwritten contract when you play a game that is meant to challenge you and stop you from winning. By winning, you succeed over the game and the rules set by the designer, and if you don't, then you lose. "Losing" has changed a lot over the years – from having to restart a game from scratch, inserting quarters to continue, to now losing in most games is just about going back to a previous save state, **roguelikes** notwithstanding.

Figure 2.2

Low-stakes games are more about personal and smaller stories, where the outcome matters directly to the character, and by extension, the player, with no penalties for messing up.

Cozy games extend from the rise in popularity of story-focused games – where instead of the player being an active participant in the events of the game, they are going for a ride and seeing where the game takes them. Many gamers criticized these games and have labeled them as "walking simulators," as that is often the extent of the gameplay.

However, as video games have evolved, so has what they can offer to someone beyond just a finger-breaking ordeal. It's undisputable at this point that video games are art, and just how there are different interpretations of what art is, there are different interpretations of a video game (Figure 2.3).

Instead of a video game testing someone with nail-biting excitement, there are games that are about experiencing a unique story that can deal with everything from depression to death in a family, cancer, and an infinite number of other topics that aren't dependent on mechanics.

Cozy games often focus on a singular mechanic that doesn't revolve around the usual progression curve of introducing more complexity and difficulty as a game goes on. It is often more about experiencing the game or the topic at hand rather than trying to "win" or "beat" the game. What makes a game cozy in the eyes of the consumer tends to differ from person to person, and in the next chapter, that will be one of the points discussed. However, there are examples that will come up throughout this book of games that are cozy but also provide advanced challenges for someone who wants to try and achieve them.

Before we start talking about how this began, I want to answer a question that some of you may be thinking – who cares about cozy games? The games that

Figure 2.3

A lot of changes have happened to games in the 2010s and early 2020s thanks to games becoming surprise hits that did not follow the traditional format of gameplay. You can have all the explosions you want in *Vampire Survivors* (A), find people seats in *Is This Seat Taken?* (B), solve a mystery in *What Remains of Edith Finch* (C), or drive across the USA in *American Truck Simulator* (D).

typically take home the top prizes each year from different outlets are those that are meant to be challenging. Looking back at The Game Awards, regardless of whether you like them or not, here are the winners from 2020 to 2025:

- 2020: *The Last of Us 2*
- 2021: *It Takes Two*
- 2022: *Elden Ring*
- 2023: *Baldur's Gate 3*
- 2024: *Astro Bot*
- 2025: *Clair Obscur: Expedition 33*

Not one of these games would be considered "cozy." However, each year, the Entertainment Software Association (ESA) continues to show that more non-gamers are playing games, and there is an underserved market for cozy games. According to the 2025 report from the ESA, 68% of people who were polled play games to relax and 62% play games to have fun.[1] As another point, cozy and wholesome games are often very accommodating towards people with disabilities, which the ESA report reports 21% of the people polled play games with a disability. Part of the growth of the game industry has been creating games that can be played by a variety of people regardless of any disabilities they might have, and why the market has grown so much over the 2010s. Designing your game around accessibility and approachability will be discussed more in Chapter 4.

Figure 2.4

Here is an example of an out-of-left-field game becoming an unexpected hit in 2025. This is a scene from *Umamusume: Pretty Derby*, a game where horse girls named after famous horses race and sing and was played and featured by a variety of streamers and managed to break through as both a mobile and PC success. I could not imagine a game like this having anywhere near the same reach 15 years ago or possibly being translated for the US market.

The stigma largely centered around calling games walking simulators has died down, and there is more room than ever before to create games more about their vibes and stories rather than about blasting monsters (Figure 2.4). For creators who are story-first, there is now more room in the market to create a story-driven game and have an audience for it. This is also why so many of the best games have come from indie developers wanting to tell something personal or create something that is purposely different from the mainstream. With that said, designing a game to be cozy or wholesome requires you to be attentive toward UI/UX and player feedback. With one exception, even though cozy games are not becoming best-sellers as the games mentioned further up, they do provide another way for designers to express themselves.

And with that, let's begin looking at the history of the genre.

Note

1 https://www.theesa.com/wp-content/uploads/2025/06/2025-Essential-Facts-Booklet-05-30-25-RGB.pdf

The Creation of the Cozy/Wholesome Market

3.1 The Origin of Casual Games

As mentioned, cozy games are an offshoot of the casual market, and it's important to briefly discuss their history and appeal before focusing on cozy. The term "casual" has changed a lot over the years, and what we consider to be the modern definition of a casual game didn't come into being until the 2000s and early 2010s with the rise of browser-based games and the mobile market (Figure 3.1). Before that, casual games were defined by those that did not revolve around combat or any high stakes gameplay, and one of the first games to break the trend of being combat-intensive was *SimCity* by Maxis and designer Will Wright (first released in 1989). The original story was that Will was creating a top-down helicopter action game where players could build little cities and bases to then attack with the helicopter, but he was having so much fun with the building aspect that he decided to make a full game out of it.

The entire *SimCity* franchise would spawn multiple games about the challenges of building and growing a city and would give birth to the city builder genre. Many city builders did have the option to play with infinite resources and not have to worry about constraints. Even though most people didn't view *SimCity* as a casual game, the next mega franchise would become one of the most popular (Figure 3.2).

DOI: 10.1201/9781003646860-3

Figure 3.1

Casual games that would come to define the market, and the term became popular thanks to the ease of playing them on mobile and browsers, and the untapped audience of non-gamers being able to experience easy-to-learn games like *Farmville* and *Angry Birds* for the first time. While this market has shrunk and changed with newer mobile games, it did punctuate changes to game design in the 2010s.

Figure 3.2

The *SimCity* franchise managed to be popular among people who wanted to build their perfectly optimized city and those that just wanted to make whatever they wanted. While *The Sims* would become the poster child for casual and sandbox games, there hasn't been a game yet that has taken away its crown.

In 2000, Maxis released *The Sims*, essentially a dollhouse simulator where players could create virtual characters or "sims" who would go about their lives with as much or as little interaction by the player as they wanted.

Both games popularized a form of gameplay that would become known as "sandbox" or "creative" mode – where any loss states are turned off, and the player is free to do and build whatever they want without any gameplay limitations. This kind of gameplay would go on to form not only the basis for a lot of casual and cozy games but offer another avenue for playing more challenging games and opening them up to a larger audience. *The Sims* would go on to have multiple games and expansions released, and there is still a healthy and vibrant audience for it well into the 2020s.

A surprising success would provide console and handheld gamers with their own take on casual games with the *Harvest Moon* series (first released in 1996 in Japan, 1997 in the USA) by Natsume. Players inherited a farm in a small countryside and were tasked to manage and grow it however they wanted. By buying seeds from the local store, players would grow crops which could be sold for money to acquire more equipment, expand their home, or add additional money makers to their farm. It was also possible to romance the local townspeople and eventually get married to have a family as well. The original series did not have any combat whatsoever or any fail states. Combat would be added to the spinoff series *Rune Factory* (first released in 2006 in Japan, 2007 in the USA). This would add in the option to go into dungeon areas to fight enemies and add more challenge and progression to the game.

The other company to get in early with the casual market would be PopCap Games. During the 2000s into the 2010s, the studio released numerous casual games through their site and casual game portals at the time. Some of their biggest successes include the *Bejeweled* series, *Peggle*, and most famously *Plants vs. Zombies* (with releases in 2000, 2007, and 2009 respectively). They managed to be one of the first developers to tap into this market of making games that were very easy to get into and approachable but had a lot of depth and gameplay to attract people who weren't normally fans of casual games (Figure 3.3). *Plants vs. Zombies* would become one of the shining examples of good GUI design, and its designer George Fan has given talks about it.

With the rise of mobile and browser-based gaming in the mid-2000s came the other avenue for casual games for non-gamers. In my *Deep Dive* looking at the mobile and free-to-play markets, this is what I referred to as the first generation of mobile and the rise of studios like Zynga and Rovio. As more people were using Facebook and the first generation of smartphones, there was suddenly a huge market of people using these technologies who did not grow up playing games. It was easier than ever to play and connect with people, and this would become more prominent over the 2010s.

With Zynga and Rovio, they became famous thanks to the successes of games like *Farmville* and *Angry Birds* (both released in 2009) respectively. *Farmville* was one of the most popular browser games and appealed to many casual fans and

Figure 3.3

For people who didn't play games in the 2000s, it's easy to overlook PopCap Games today, but during this decade, they were one of the premier casual game developers, and the successes of *Plants vs. Zombies* (A) and *Peggle* (B) brought them into mainstream notoriety, on top of the numerous successful casual games.

non-gamers at the time. *Angry Birds* succeeded thanks to its easy to learn, difficult to master gameplay. Following the success, it would spawn numerous spinoffs, sequels, and movies through the 2010s. It would not be until the middle of the 2010s that the mobile space fully changed to start appealing to core and hardcore gamers and enter the second generation of mobile design; for more on that, please read *Game Design Deep Dive: Free to Play Games.*

Browser-based gaming was popularized by the fact that these games were built around real-world timers, meaning that it would take actual minutes, hours, or days for things to progress. Instead of having to factor in time to play, these games were popular for logging on to play for a few minutes, setting things to run automatically, and then revisiting them when the timers were up. Thanks to the simple gameplay, it meant that they could be extended almost indefinitely with new content and goals to reach, and there were people who played browser games daily for months or years at their peak. Despite the casual atmosphere, many popular browser games were designed around guild vs. guild content, which are player groups fighting against each other, with people competing to see whose guild could become the best on the server.

During the 2000s, there was also the boom of the massively multiplayer online game market (MMOG). Most of these games were designed around high-stakes combat and the thrill of victory or the sting of losing equipment and progress for failing. However, long before casual gamers and the casual market was defined, there were people who played these games focusing on the low-stakes content – crafting

Figure 3.4

The 2000s for the MMOG genre was all about turning as many popular properties into MMOGs as possible. The vast majority of them are no longer around, but some are still popular, such as *Lord of the Rings Online* (left) and *Dungeons and Dragons Online* (right). While their combat systems are dated, the highlight still remains being able to explore these worlds as your own personal character.

and selling items. A popular form of playing these games was "roleplay servers," where players would play them as if they were the actual characters in the world (Figure 3.4). While this kind of gameplay was considered secondary for the majority of MMOGs, there were a few that only focused on low-stakes and social interactions.

A Tale in the Desert (first released in 2003) by Egenesis centered on crafting in ancient Egypt. Players could craft goods and buy and sell them within the in-game economy. There was no combat in the game, with challenges built around constructing structures and what the community could accomplish. Unlike other MMOGs, the game would update with new additions and changes in the form of a "telling" every 18 months that also resets the world. As of early 2026, the game is on its 11th telling.

Second Life by Linden Lab was released in 2003 and was designed to be a social MMOG. Players could interact with people from all around the world and create goods that could be bought and sold between them. It is also one of the few MMOGs, and just video games in general, where players could exchange the in-game currency for real money. To this day, with the MMOGs that are still available to play, there are communities who focus on the social and non-combat portions of the gameplay.

Nintendo would also have a hand in bringing casual games to the consoles with the *Animal Crossing* series (first released in 2001). In it, players become residents of a village of animals and can go about their business collecting items, furnishing their home, and paying back the debt of their landlord: Tom Nook. The game also came with the ability to play classic Nintendo games on a Nintendo console within the world itself. While the players had a long-term goal of repaying Tom Nook, they were free to take as long as they wanted. Like *The Sims*, *Animal Crossing* was completely open-ended, and the player was never at risk of failing. The series would go on to have multiple games released, with the latest one as of writing this book: – *New Horizons* in 2020 –, doing exceptionally well thanks to becoming the go-to game for people to play during the COVID-19 lockdowns.

In 2004, PlayStation 2 would get one of the more surprisingly popular casual games with *Katamari Damacy* by Namco and designed by Keita Takahashi. In it, players controlled the son of the "King of All Cosmos" who must roll a giant ball around collecting junk and other items to turn into stars. Instead of button presses, the game used the twin analog sticks on the PS2 controller to simulate pushing and maneuvering the ball. With a great soundtrack and distinct visuals, the game would go on to have multiple sequels, and he would continue to design other games after leaving Namco. As of 2025, Takahashi has since moved into indie development and released more cozy games such as *Wattam* and *To a T* (released in 2019 and 2025 respectively).

While browser games have declined in the 2010s, one of the more popular ones is still going with *Fallen London* by Failbetter Games. Released in 2009, the game is about exploring and living in an alternate London that sank beneath the Earth and now exists underground in another realm full of creatures and mysterious deities. The player decides which actions they want to undertake each day, which in turn will progress in different storylines and unlock new items and skills that can be used to move further in the world. The game's setting and variety of storylines and characters helped its audience grow over the years. Failbetter would extend the universe with *Sunless Sea* and *Sunless Skies* in 2015 and 2019 respectively, both focusing on real-time action-adventure gameplay and not browser design.

An advantage of casual and cozy games is being able to reach a market that is normally undersold games, and the studio Artifex Mundi in the 2010s capitalized on this with their series of adventure and hidden object games. These games were often aimed at women and casual gamers and featured low-stakes stories with a female protagonist. While there were puzzles to solve, the game would provide hints or just allow someone to skip a puzzle if they didn't want to do it.

The appeal to women with casual games is not exclusive to Artifex Mundi; there are other series and studios who have catered to this market with their own examples that will be discussed later in this chapter.

Returning to sandbox and creative gameplay, another massive success that would create its own subgenre came out officially in 2011 with *Minecraft by* Mojang Studios (Figure 3.5). The player was dropped into a procedurally generated world and then given free rein to do whatever they wanted in it. The game would be the first hugely popular take on the "survival crafter" subgenre – where players must build and survive in a variety of locales. The entire progression curve of *Minecraft*

Figure 3.5

Minecraft has graduated from being a video game to a cultural milestone, and this caption isn't big enough to highlight how much it has touched over the 2010s. For many people, it's also their first exposure to procedural generation every time a world is created. If I do a book on survival crafting at some point, it will definitely be one of the games focused on for its impact on the genre.

revolved around gathering resources, to create better tools for exploring, to get more resources, to build more tools, and repeat.

The world generation was designed so that the surface layer is the safest with the basic resources readily available all around, but of course that hasn't stopped people from making underground cities. As players dig deeper, they will find the materials needed to produce better tools and equipment to help them get further.

By laying blocks down, players could create literally any kind of structure they wanted – from a simple shack to an entire mansion, to even people recreating famous locales and places like the Death Star. The early versions of the game focused solely on the creative aspects, but over the years, more content focused on progression and exploring the different depths of the world was released. *Minecraft* in 2025 is a completely different beast compared to its humble origins, and has gone on to spawn spinoffs, launch the careers of YouTubers and streamers, and had a movie released in 2025.

The appeal of *Minecraft*'s creative mode would be seen in just about every survival crafter released since. Just as there is an audience for people who want to survive in brutal conditions and live off scant resources, there are people who just want to create the ultimate base, apartment, cabin, castle, spaceship, and many more. The only game that has come close to the success and reach of *Minecraft* for younger audiences and creative people has been *Roblox* (first released in 2006 by

Roblox Corporation). Players can play and create their own games, and even sell them and other created items. It has also had controversies over the years revolving around not protecting minors, and as of 2026, there are different lawsuits filed by individual states against the company.

While many cozy games fall into the casual category, not every casual game would be considered cozy, and this has led to debates and arguments from fans and creators online about what it means to make a cozy game that will be coming up later in the book.

Most cozy games went largely unnoticed outside of the indie space, and the market for cozy games changed dramatically from the start of the 2010s to the end.

3.2 Curating Cozy (and Wholesome) Games of the 2010s

The 2010s was a decade defined by indie studios coming into their own, and outside of *Animal Crossing*, almost every other major example of a cozy or wholesome game would come from indie studios. As with previous *Deep Dives*, when it's time to list games of the chosen genre, trying to catalogue every cozy and wholesome game released in the 2010s is impossible. Not only are we talking about subgenres which are niche, but many of these games were never released on Steam and are only available on the site Itch.io or directly from the developer. An example being most visual novel games that have explored everything from cozy and mature topics, sexuality, and much more.

The reach and impact of indie games are some of the major trends that changed over the 2010s. Two early examples of games that did lead to mainstream acclaim while focusing on storytelling were *To the Moon* and *Dear Esther*.

Released in 2011 by Freebird Games, *To the Moon* told the story of a company that helps people fulfill their dying wish by going into their memories and making artificial memories of what they wanted to achieve in life (Figure 3.6). The game explored a lot of mature concepts that other games were not touching at the time – from accepting death and tragedy, mental illness, to a life unfulfilled. This was more impressive by being one of the first mainstream games built using the program *RPG Maker*, which is an editor/engine predominantly used to create role-playing games (RPGs). Despite that, *To the Moon* did not focus on turn-based combat and was all about the story. Over the 2010s, *RPG Maker*'s popularity and acceptance would grow thanks to more experimental and mature RPGs developed with it. Freebird created two sequels with *Finding Paradise* and *Impostor Factory* in 2017 and 2021 respectively along with spinoffs and smaller games, and there is a finale in the works.

With *Dear Esther* (released commercially in 2012 by The Chinese Room), players explored an island while hearing narration by a man reading letters to his deceased wife. There was no combat, and the game focused on learning more about the story. *Dear Esther* would also lead to a new term being coined with "walking simulators" by gamers used to describe games that the player can only walk around while the story is unfolding around them. Despite the negative, this

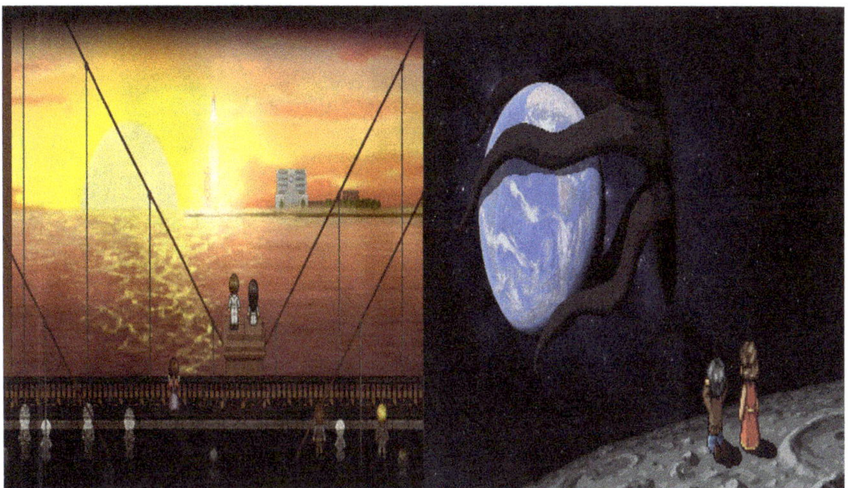

Figure 3.6

The entire story from Freebird Games is an amazing narrative told through the medium of video games, and *To the Moon* was one of the first games to be promoted and talked about solely for its story. There are plenty of people (including me) who have cried from some of the scenes that I won't be spoiling in this book. The games do an excellent job of weaving comedy, tragedy, and hope, throughout each one. (Games shown are *To the Moon* and *Impostor Factory*)

style of storytelling would become popularized for story-driven games, and many short-form horror titles were released in the 2010s.

One of the most successful games released from the indie space was *Stardew Valley* (released in 2016 by Eric Barone and his studio Concerned Ape). In interviews, Eric talked about wanting an experience like *Harvest Moon* that was not ported to the PC at the time (Figure 3.7). While the basics of the *Harvest Moon* experience were here, *Stardew Valley* greatly expanded on all the content. The player's farm could be further customized with additional services and far greater personalization options. The player's character could romance far more people compared to *Harvest Moon* and would also have progression in terms of new skills. By performing different tasks such as farming, fishing, fighting, etc., players could level up in said tasks and unlock new options and equipment related to them.

Like *Rune Factory*, *Stardew Valley* featured combat in the form of exploring procedurally generated dungeons to acquire bonus resources and additional items. Said resources could then either be used to create new gear for further exploration or sell the materials for money that could be used to upgrade the farm. As of 2026, Eric's next game *Haunted Chocolatier* is in development but does not have a release date at the time of this book's draft, and *Stardew Valley* is still seeing updates from time-to-time. *Stardew Valley's* design was a watershed moment for cozy games and the entire farming genre, and I will be going into more detail about the design in Section 3.4.

Figure 3.7

This is the start of the many images from *Stardew Valley* that will be shown in this book, and you'll be able to see how my farm and character changed over the course of my play.

Stardew Valley's success would lead to many more farming-style games being released. Sometimes, these games may involve a farm, but not in the traditional sense, such as 2017's *Slime Rancher* by Monomi Park. In it, the player must manage a "slime ranch" by finding, raising, and taking care of a variety of different slimes. By feeding and keeping them happy, the player would earn "plorts" which could either be sold for money or used to crossbreed slimes into new species. Progress was tied to selling the plorts to buy new gear and getting past giant versions of slimes to reach new areas and treasures. A sequel was released in 2025 that expanded on the gameplay with more to explore and more slimes to catch.

Making a game in 3D regardless of the genre will always be more challenging than a 2D alternative, and there have been a few successful cozy games to go in this direction. Besides *Slime Rancher*, there are the games in the *My Time* series, with the releases of *My Time at Portia* (2019), *My Time at Sandrock* (2023), and *My Time at Evershine* (in development at the time of drafting), all by Pathea Games. The series is a popular take on another kind of subgenre – life simulator/RPG or simulation RPG. Players in these games are free to explore, interact with a variety of people, and perform different jobs. Each job is a complete system with its own progression, mechanics, and tasks to go with it. Like *Stardew Valley*, the player is free to engage or ignore the different jobs at their leisure, with progress tied to exploring and figuring out more about the world itself, but to discover everything, the player will have to make use of all the different jobs.

In Section 5.5, I will be expanding on how the same game system can be used to create vastly different experiences. A popular pastime for indie developers and

Figure 3.8

Grey Alien Games' lineup all have the same foundation, but as you can see with these screenshots, they are very different interpretations of solitaire. Part of the challenge of experimenting was figuring out what their audience was looking for, *Shadowhand* (top-right) for many was too difficult with its combat, while *Ancient Enemy* (bottom-left) scaled back the complexity to make it easier to learn.

first-time designers is taking a classic game and putting a twist on it to create a different way of playing it. A studio that has managed to do this in terms of both cozy and challenging is Grey Alien Games ran by Jake Birkett and Helen Carmichael, who have been making casual games since the 2000s (Figure 3.8). One of their bigger successes in the cozy/casual space was *Regency Solitaire* (released in 2015). Taking place in the regency era of Britain, the game tells a charming story between solitaire levels. Players must remove all the cards on the field to win, and the game has different difficulty settings for those who want a challenge. Instead of just playing straight solitaire, players can unlock special abilities and items that allow them to control the board and their own cards when the time is right. The studio would explore further twists on the solitaire formula with *Shadowhand* (released in 2017) that featured combat tied to solitaire, the duo, alongside Night Signal Entertainment, released Forbidden Solitaire in 2026; with a focus on combining solitaire with horror.

Part of the appeal of combining cozy and idle design is being able to create a low-stakes experience that can scale upward and outward with new content and goals to achieve, and the most famous example of this pairing is *Forager* by HopFrog (released in 2019). The game's original concept was developed in a game jam, and it proved so popular in it that the designer turned it into a full game. The player's task is to explore islands looking for new treasures, challenges, and resources. The location of each island is randomly shuffled when the game starts, but the player will always start out on the same basic one. Resources will have to be gathered by hand at first, but the player will eventually get the ability to automate the process.

Unlike *Stardew Valley* where progression is free-formed and nonlinear, *Forager* requires the player to level up to unlock the appearance of new resources, new machines, and quality of life features to become available. The idle design comes into play with how scaling works. The most apparent way of progressing is unlocking new islands, but the cost gets progressively more expensive the further the player goes from the starting island. This will require more effective ways of earning money, which in turn will also require the player to upgrade their tools and abilities to do more in the world. There is combat, puzzles, and many goals to achieve if someone wants to complete it 100%.

Another area where cozy and wholesome games can excel at is being able to tell interesting and emotional stories, as with *To the Moon* mentioned earlier. In 2020, two story-driven games were released to critical acclaim with *Coffee Talk* and *Spiritfarer* (by Toge Productions and Thunder Lotus Games respectively). *Coffee Talk* is about the player running a coffee shop and interacting with the different customers who come in and learning more about their lives while making sure to get their order right. The game focused on the conversations, and there were no stakes regarding managing the shop. In a way, *Coffee Talk* would serve as a different way of presenting a visual novel story to players – the "job" of the game is there to give the player something to do and frame the story, but the focus is on the storytelling and worldbuilding. This format would go on to inspire a variety of games released since, with a sequel released in 2023.

Spiritfarer by Thunder Lotus Games focuses on coming to terms with saying goodbye to loved ones. As Stella, it's your job to find the lost souls of Stella's loved ones in the afterlife and take care of them before they are ready to move on. The player will explore the ocean, perform different mini-games, and do their best to keep everyone as happy as they can be – another game where there are no stakes, with the focus on exploring the world and learning more about the people Stella is helping.

A surprising and emotional hit was *Unpacking* by Witch Beam (released in 2021). The game followed a person as they moved from different homes and apartments over the course of their life. In each stage, all the player had to do was find places to store the different items that they brought with them. The game earned a following thanks to its low-stakes play and the deeper story that could be understood from the different items and where the character is moving to in each stage.

Given the appeal of *The Sims* with letting the player personalize in a relaxing setting, it wouldn't be long in the 2010s until a cozy version of this would come out with "diorama"-styled games (Figure 3.9). These games are all about full personalization of a space without any resource or gameplay limitations. This specific style has seen all manner of variety: from small ones where you create a garden, to ones where you construct a town, building, or anything else. They will typically not feature any progression or goals, and it is all about creating something in the space.

Figure 3.9

The diorama style focuses entirely on being able to personalize a space. While they're not as popular in the mainstream market, they do have a fanbase much in the same way as people showing off their homes and characters in a game like *The Sims* or *Animal Crossing*. The games shown are *Summerhouse* (released in 2024 by Friedemann) and *Gourdlets* (released in 2024 by AuntyGames)

A popular trend from the indie space in the 2010s was creating short-form games, which can focus on either unique gameplay or telling a story. One of the more popular examples in the cozy space was *A Short Hike* by Adam Robinson-Yu released in 2019. In it, players are trying to reach the peak of a popular mountain tourist spot. While the game can be finished in less than an hour, there are plenty of side activities and places to explore off the beaten path to extend the playtime. This is expanded on either by finding different items that can unlock new paths or by acquiring golden feathers that allow the main character to fly and climb further.

In yet another subgenre that has seen popularity among different playstyles, we have "insert job here" simulators. Each game is about performing the job of said title as accurately and realistically as possible, even with some taking place in fantasy environments. Driving became one of the more popular jobs to build games around, such as truck driving with a variety of them from the studio SCS Software. In these games, the player will drive around accurate representations of cities and streets to deliver cargo, managing their truck and trying not to rear-end anyone. The games from SCS Software have seen continued support by releasing downloadable content (**DLC**) expansions that add more cities and places to go.

The oldest example of this style would be *Microsoft Flight Simulator* (first released in 1982; latest release in 2024). Players are challenged not only to learn how to fly a plane but to fly a variety of planes across the globe with simulated weather. The series has been celebrated for the level of detail and allows anyone to experience the thrill of flying a plane, albeit a digital version.

The combination of video game progression with the low stakes of doing everyday jobs has created a hit-or-miss subgenre, as you never know which job is going to become popular. Speaking of, here are two examples that blew up in 2025 and 2026 that couldn't be further apart from each other. First, there is *Schedule One* by TVGS that focuses on the player becoming a drug manufacturer and dealer in a small town. While the second one is just getting traction in early 2026 with *Retro Rewind: Video Store Simulator* by Blood Pact Studios. In it, players have to grow and manage a video store like Blockbuster Videos from the 90's. Both games are in early access at the time of drafting this book.

Just as there are casual examples, there are simulator games meant to be challenging and intricate affairs. An infamous example is *My Summer Car* by Amistech Games (released in 2025). The game tasks the player to fully restore a car while earning enough money to live and hopefully not crash and destroy all their hard work. The opposite of a casual experience, the game is self-described as a "life survival simulator," tasking the player to fully understand how a car works and rebuild the car of their nightmares from the ground up.

With this subgenre, one of the most popular ones was *PowerWash Simulator* (released in 2022 by Futurlab) (Figure 3.10). The player's job is to use a power washer to clean various buildings and vehicles around a town. Progression comes in the form of earning stars which are used to unlock new tools to buy and more areas to clean in. The main story mode has no stakes or limitations for the player

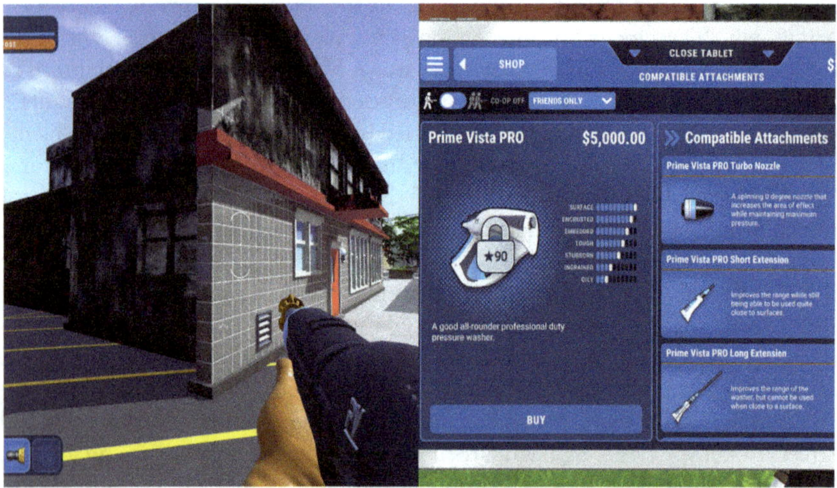

Figure 3.10

PowerWash Simulator is another game that surprised everyone with how it blew up. The combination of low stakes and relaxing gameplay, and how it drip feeds progression in the form of new power washers worked. It's a great game to study in terms of approachability features and keeping people engaged, right down to the "ding" noise that plays each time something is fully cleaned.

to worry about, while the challenge mode can throw additional conditionals at them. The game has been expanded multiple times with tie-ins to other properties and more maps introduced. As of 2025, a sequel is in development and can currently be played in early access.

PowerWash Simulator worked by recontextualizing first-person shooting (FPS) mechanics into the power washing. Watching an area that was previously completely covered in dirt and rust and now being squeaky clean is motivating. The story mode was designed so that anyone could play it, with the use of the power washer being intuitive to use. Progression was tied to buying new equipment which would allow the player to clean the different surfaces more easily but not to change or alter the main task of cleaning.

An aspect of the rise and appeal of indie development was a chance to tell stories and experiences that weren't possible at the AAA level, with many cozy and wholesome games following suit. 2023's *Venba* by Visai Games follows a South Indian family living in Canada that connects through recipes handed down from parent to child. The gameplay focused on figuring out the recipes to cook for each scene to move the story along.

Environmentalism has been a topic featured in many games, especially "edutainment" titles aimed at kids. With *Spilled* (released in 2024 by Lenti), the short-form game has players cleaning up lakes that have been polluted, recycling the trash to earn money to upgrade their boat, and repeating it level by level. As with the other games mentioned in this section, *Spilled* was not designed to be overly challenging or a lengthy experience, but the wholesome message and story of the developer quitting school to work on it resonated with people to help fund their kickstarter.

Being able to look at mental health is another positive for wholesome games, and *Wanderstop* by Ivy Road (released in 2025) focuses on a warrior struggling with PTSD and panic attacks following a traumatic incident in their life after losing an important fight. To recover, they decide to work at a magic tea shop, with the gameplay centered on growing herbs and other ingredients to preparing tea for different guests.

There haven't been too many examples of cozy games from AAA studios to discuss, but there are a few to talk about., *Fantasy Life i: The Girl Who Steals Time* (released in 2025 by Level 5) is a sequel to the original *Fantasy Life* released on the Nintendo 3DS in 2012. Like *Stardew Valley*, the player has different jobs that they can do in the world, but *Fantasy Life* embellishes each job with different rules and systems, and the player can swap between them when they see fit.

Nintendo has also scored another major hit for cozy and *Pokémon* fans with *Pokémon Pokopia* released in 2026 (developed by Omega Force and Game Freak). Players control a Ditto, who must rebuild the world and create homes for a variety of Pokémon. The ability to customize and personalize the player's world continues to resonate with people much like *Animal Crossing: New Horizons* did.

A newer trend for cozy games started in 2024 with a redesign of the idle genre. The limited input and low stakes have always made the genre a great cozy example.

Figure 3.11

Quarter-view idle games are one of the most brilliant ideas I've seen for the genre in a long time and are a great example of fixing something that wasn't even a problem for most people who play these games, to make them even easier to experience. These games are just a few of the many that have shown up since the release of *Rusty*. (Games Shown: A: *Ropuka's Idle Island*, B: *Maltese's Fluffy Onsen*, C: *Rusty's Retirement*, D: *Nanomon Virtual Pet*)

While idle games have evolved into more demanding takes with the "incremental" variety, there is also a new generation of cozy idle games with "quarter view" idle, with the first take being *Rusty's Retirement* by Mr. Morris Games (Figure 3.11). The game only takes up literally a quarter of someone's monitor and follows a robot named Rusty who is enjoying retirement while working on his farm. The player's interaction involves buying new seeds, buildings, and robotic helpers to assist Rusty. What's ingenious about the design is how it cuts out the middleman in a manner of speaking. Many people who play idle games will keep it running in the background while they do other tasks; the quarter view means that the player can keep watching the game at the same time as they are doing other tasks, along with listening to peaceful music. Just like *Stardew Valley*, the success has led to many other quarter-view idle games being released or in development as of 2026.

The 2010s also brought with it the rise in popularity of visual novels, in no small part thanks to the availability of the publicly available tool Twine. From cute to gruesome, happy to dark, there are hundreds if not thousands of visual novel games. To even try to list them all is an impossible task, with many of the smaller ones only available on Itch.io. Visual novels focus on storytelling and, despite their popularity, are off-topic for this book on game design as they are more about writing than creating gameplay.

While cozy and wholesome games started out as an exception to more mainstream genres and designs, its acceptance as a legitimate genre for the larger market would come with help from the creation of Wholesome Direct.

3.3 The Wholesome Games Movement

The 2010s was a very chaotic time for the game industry, to say the least. With the rise of indie development that has punctuated almost every *Deep Dive* I've written, to the horrible attacks and vitriol from the supporters of "Gamergate," what a video game is and what it would become changed over the decade.

As I said in the last chapter, there was a stigma from gamers surrounding games that focused on storytelling over gameplay. Even the major successes that broke out, like *Dear Esther* and *To the Moon*, didn't have a lot of staying power after their initial successes reaching a new audience. *Stardew Valley's* success led to many imitators and developers chasing after it, but many cozy games were not reaching mainstream audiences the same way for the rest of the 2010s.

In 2019, designer Matthew Taylor began curating games that he felt were "wholesome." The idea was to shine a spotlight on games that would appeal to people outside of the traditional market of violent, high-stakes, or stress-inducing games (Figure 3.12). Games that could be enjoyed by anyone and have low to no stakes for the player. This would also begin the trend of categorizing games as wholesome, where they were previously just defined by their gameplay. Over the

Figure 3.12

Wholesome Direct has done a great job of providing a centralized collection of wholesome games for consumers to see and is but one of many themed festivals and showcases on Steam each year.

years, this would grow into a community of wholesome gamers and developers, events and festivals to show off more games, and became a way of proving to everyone that there were more games out there to play that weren't focusing on violence or dark subject matters. Since then, there has been a yearly Wholesome Direct festival on Steam to show off these games to a larger market with more wholesome and cozy games being released yearly.

> Many people see wholesome games as a sudden response to an increasingly unstable, violent world. But if you talk to players, you'll quickly learn that many of us have always enjoyed these kinds of experiences and wanted more. Only recently, with the rise of indie games, have those players truly been catered to. And slowly but surely, larger studios and publishers are starting to take note.
>
> – **Matthew Taylor**

With more people playing games today than they did before, we have seen massive changes to the demographics and reach of video games thanks to the popularity of indie games showing that there are fans who are interested in cozy and wholesome games. The indie scene is the reason why having a wholesome game market even exists in the first place, as per Matthew's statement above. For every game mentioned in the previous section, there are still countless more that have been released or are being developed. Each year, Wholesome Direct will take submissions from developers who want to include their game in the event. For more about Wholesome Direct, and if you want to submit a game to the event, you can check out the website: https://wholesomegames.com/

3.4 Studying the Success of *Stardew Valley*

Every game genre will have that one title or franchise that goes on to define it and be the breakout success, and *Stardew Valley* would set the stage for so many cozy, wholesome, and low-stakes games to come (Figure 3.13).

I already discussed the basics in Section 3.2, but I want to focus more on the design and how it succeeded.

Stardew Valley is one of the most popular examples of a style of game known as "slice of life" – focusing on the player living day to day without the high stakes and world exploration of other games. Instead of exploring a wide-open world, these games will usually focus on a few areas. The previous major example would be *Animal Crossing*, and there are many indie games that have used this style, not just in the cozy genre. While there is technically an end and goals to pursue, they are optional for the player to experience the world one in-game day at a time.

Instead of focusing on long-term progression and an end goal, the game goes for smaller and easier to reach goals that push the player forward in different ways. As mentioned, each one of the game's primary tasks – farming, fishing, combat, mining, and foraging, can be upgraded through use. Lesser games that use this approach tend to only focus on separate goals – the player must produce 100 apples or fight 50 rats: with no connection or rewards between them. Here, each

Figure 3.13

Without a doubt, *Stardew Valley* is the banner game to be mentioned when talking about cozy and wholesome games. Its success, as I'm about to discuss, was about refining the farming sim genre that was unheard of on PC at the time and growing every aspect of it.

path connects and embellishes the other four, so that there is a reason or benefit for doing the other paths.

Let's take farming as a quick example. By growing crops, the player is rewarded with money that can be used to buy supplies or upgrades to assist with the other paths. Food can be cooked into meals that provide more energy each day and limited-time bonuses for different paths. To grow the farm, the player is going to need a combination of new machines and structures that have their own resources. Machines will require the player to gather construction materials via scavenging, finding crystals, and creating different metal bars from mining. The best way to get the ore needed is by going into the combat sections, with better ore the further down the player goes. On top of that, the player can upgrade most of their tools by spending money and materials at the blacksmith, which improves their utility. Fishing provides an easy way to gather ingredients for meals; some machines are related to it or sell for money to buy for other resources.

There is always something the player can do, and in response, they will be rewarded (Figure 3.14). A common trap from other games is when the player is required to do something with no benefit other than moving things along. In this case, the reward for doing work is simply doing even more work. With *Stardew Valley*, when a new building or resource is introduced, that comes with new features that make use of it to add more to the game. What you don't want to see is that a new resource is just what the player has been doing previously but now it is slower to use.

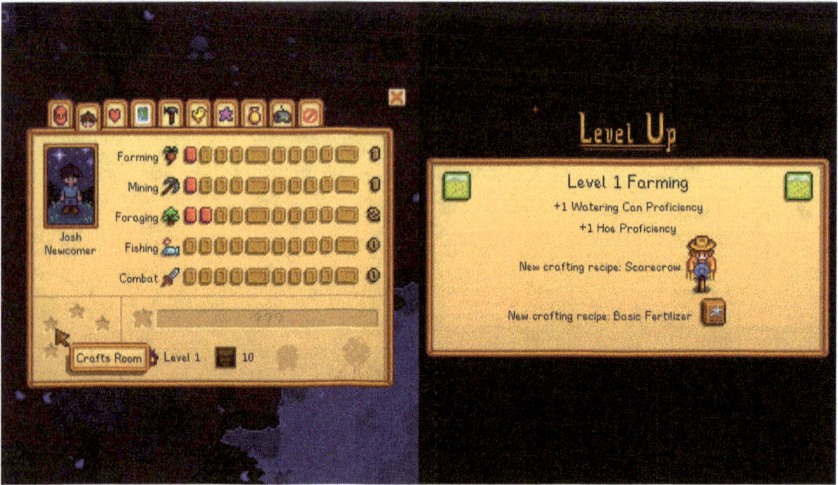

Figure 3.14

Each skill path in the game provides the player with the means of earning money and seeing more in the world. While the standard route is to eventually max out all the skills listed here, there are people who have done challenges only focusing on one to earn all the money they need, and the game is flexible enough to be played in different ways.

For crafting-style games, we like to refer to the different materials and refined goods as tiers – the higher the tier, the more resources and progress in the overall game are required to produce them. A base example is moving from common tools to bronze, silver, gold, etc., which the game provides to make it easier to perform the respective tasks. From a progression and game design standpoint, good examples of tiers change how production works and provides new rewards and items for completing them. Higher-tiered goods in *Stardew Valley* beyond the initial crops include making jams, wine, raising livestock, and more. They each have their own different processes to produce them and reward the player with far more money as a result. The game did a great job of moving the player forward with new things to produce, without it becoming a chore or frustrating to do. A poor example would be something like this:

Wooden Bed

- Cost 100 wood
- 40 seconds to produce
- Sells for 50 gold

Copper Bed

- Cost 200 copper
- 90 seconds to produce
- Sells for 120 gold

Even though the copper bed makes more gold, it takes more resources and time to produce, and nothing is different about the process itself. Creating an engaging progression curve for cozy games will be elaborated on in Section 5.4.

Due to the interconnected nature of needing different resources and goods at various progression points, the game goes out of its way to provide different means of collecting the raw materials, with the simplest one being money. The player can purchase different tiers of resources as opposed to having to go out and collect them from the world. At the start, wood and stone are going to be needed in heavy supply to fund the construction of the different buildings. While the player can go out and chop trees or break up stones respectively, they could just buy whatever they need from Robin, who runs the store that constructs new buildings.

This change in how someone acquires goods is an important aspect of the progression curve of playing *Stardew* or any construction/building style game. What you don't want is to force the player to repeat tasks the same way when they are beyond that point in terms of progression. This can be viewed as a punishment by making things take longer the further the player is. By the point in *Stardew* when the player has enough money to be able to just purchase goods, this provides the player with a money sink so that they will still have a use for money far into the late game. A tedious part of farming is having to spend a portion of the day watering all the crops (except for the rainy days) which eats into the amount of available time the player can be doing other tasks. One of the early unlocks that go with farming is being able to create sprinklers that will water fields surrounding the sprinkler daily. With enough sprinklers set, the player will never have to water a single crop ever again.

One of the many objectives the player can go after is to fill the community center with many different produced and scavenged items, which provides another incentive for doing everything (Figure 3.15). Another option is to side with the mega store Joja Mart, which will tear down the community center. Instead of making progress through donating resources, players can spend more money to open the paths and bonus structures if they choose this route.

Given the interconnected nature of the game, there are people who will go for mastering all the paths and seeing all the content, which requires interacting with both combat and the resource production sides. Unlike other games of this style, the player is not required to engage with combat if they choose. While it will help them get access to resources easier, it is possible to once again purchase essential materials from the different vendors if the player prefers to. Twice a week, a merchant shows up who will sell rarer items, including harder to catch fish, allowing someone to complete tasks without having to do those specific systems.

Figure 3.15

The community center, when the game was first released, was the only real goal the game had. Completing the different bundles would provide the player with useful, and in some cases, required unlocks to do more. The bundles required goods from all professions, which also serves to further incentivize the player to do everything. Today, it is the requirement to access *Stardew Valley*'s new end-game content.

This next point may sound surprising to the uninitiated, but *Stardew Valley* is one of the few examples in this space to provide long-term events and situations. Most farming games will have at minimum a day and night cycle, with resources and other situations different depending on the time of day. What *Stardew Valley* did, like both *Harvest Moon* and *Animal Crossing*, is present a world that is moving forward day to day. Shops will have sales from time to time or be closed on certain days. The townspeople have birthdays, and the town itself will put on major festivals every few weeks that become an all-day break from the regular gameplay (Figure 3.16). The use of seasons means that the crops the player can grow and sell will change.

For the overall story, certain events are set to happen at specific points, with the game now having multiple in-game years' worth of content to explore. Once the player hits year 2, the price of basic goods will go up to match how much more money the player is making at that point. What is considered the normal ending of the game can happen at the beginning of year 3, when the player is visited by the spirit of their grandfather. By completing enough tasks, they can earn "perfection" and get a statue commemorating the event. The ultimate goal, and what players consider to be the "true end" of playing the game is reaching 100% completion. This requires completing every task, collecting/producing every good, and other conditionals. For most people, 100% is a step too far for a cozy game, but this does provide everyone with something to aim for.

Figure 3.16

It's surprising how many of the farming sims and slice of life games that have come out after *Stardew Valley* ignored this aspect of the worldbuilding. Part of the reason for the longevity of the game is how people connect with the characters and the town itself as a place they want to continue visiting. The game even goes as far as to have certain days where shops are closed, along with the myriads of random events that can happen to surprise the player.

Stardew Valley does a great job of threading the needle between having a low-stakes vibe, while lightly slapping the player's wrist if they mess up. The most common mistake is not keeping track of their character's energy meter and having it reach 0. The character will become exhausted and will move far slower. If the player keeps using energy, they will pass out; the same will happen if the character is still awake past 2 AM. The punishment is that the player will recover less energy the next day, and they will lose some money. If the player is defeated while fighting, they will drop a few items and will be rushed to the hospital. The player can pay a fee to the adventurer's guild to have them recover the items. There are no long-term consequences for messing up, and any energy penalties go away the following morning.

One aspect that has since been copied by other games is the interaction between the player and the townsfolk. With the player's character not speaking, the different people are the players' only way of learning about the world and life in the town. Each person has a different background and behavior during the day. It is possible to romance certain characters who can then become your bride or groom. Over the years, the number of characters that the player can wed has been increased through updates. By befriending everyone, the player can also see special cutscenes for reaching certain friendship milestones.

Good characterizations and writing are another way that cozy and wholesome games can touch people, and *Stardew Valley* would set another trend in this respect. There have been countless visual novel and dating simulation games over the years, but *Stardew Valley*, for many people who didn't play those games, was the first time they could play a game like this and grow to love hanging out with the various characters.

Part of the longevity and interest in *Stardew Valley* has been helped by the consistent updates the game has had since its release. The current version at the time of drafting this book is 1.6.15, released in December 2024, and there was an announcement of a planned 1.7 update coming out. These updates have done everything ranging from adding new crops and events, improving the graphics, fixing bugs, and even adding multiplayer and new starting farms. A major addition added with later versions was the new mastery challenges that open once the player hits the max level with each skill. These additional unlocks require a lot of experience but reward the player with a game-changing upgrade for each job.

And all this is on top of the bevy of mods that fans have been creating for the game: adding new characters, quality of life elements, new products, and much more. The best games will often transcend their release and development with support from their fandom, and I don't see people becoming tired of *Stardew Valley* anytime soon.

In the order of these *Deep Dives*, this book comes after Metroidvanias, and in it, I said that *Hollow Knight* was the undisputed best-selling example of the genre; outpacing all the other games combined. *Stardew Valley* according to Steam Spy[1] sits at between 20 to 50 million copies sold just on Steam itself, with other sites estimating it at 41 million copies across all platforms, making it one of the bestselling single-player games of the 2010s and easily one of the bestselling indie games of all time.

What is even more amazing about the success is that *Stardew Valley* managed to capture the same spark that *Plants vs. Zombies* did – it is a game that was not aimed at hardcore gamers, but the appeal and gameplay transcended the market. Just as you can play the game very relaxed, there are people who have done speed run challenges and set extreme goals for playing it. The number of ways to speed-run the game, and by extension, categories of challenges, has become its own microcosm of YouTubers and streamers all trying to outdo each other in different ways.

Some updates have added in more endgame content that tests how well the player has been producing the different goods and earning money. A brand-new area in the form of Ginger Island is unlocked after finishing the community center or unlocking all the projects with Joja Mart (Figure 3.17). The island provides a new area to explore, one more dungeon to fight through, new crops and collectible resources, and paves the way for players to attempt even harder challenges once they are ready.

There is a great "just one more day" flow state to this game, as each new day brings with it the allure of getting more resources, finally being able to afford a new upgrade, or just interacting with your favorite townsfolk. While there is an official

Figure 3.17

The addition of Ginger Island provides players with a new goal to aim for. The island's growth is based on finding golden walnuts and, once developed, it becomes another ecosystem and potential moneymaker, along with the pursuit of 100%.

end to the story of the game, that hasn't stopped people from continuing to play past it and for some to go after 100%.

The multiple ways of playing are also worth mentioning. Outside of aiming for max completion, the player's goals are going to be centered around purchasing new items and structures which cost gold. How the player acquires gold is entirely up to them – do they fish all day? Find rare jewels while mining to sell? Grow tons of crops, and so on. There is no one "correct" way to play, and that goes with the low stakes and cozy design.

The legacy of *Stardew Valley* can be seen with the increased number of slice of life games that have been released, becoming the poster child for cozy games, and why there have been so many farming-related games developed since.

3.5 The Appeal of Cozy and Wholesome Games

Cozy/wholesome games exist in their own market compared to traditional games and genres, and there are several parts of the appeal and understanding of the consumer base for them.

As I said earlier, cozy games are meant to be low stakes and not have any stress playing them. Since they are also part of the casual game market, cozy games are also very easy to learn, making them appealing to non-gamers or first-timers looking for something to do. Wholesome games are about a specific feel to them meant to uplift the person playing them.

While everyone handles stress differently, there are plenty of people out there who prefer to do something relaxing after a hard day's work, and cozy and wholesome games, such as *Animal Crossing: New Horizons*, are a perfect way to de-stress. And to that point, many of these games focus on one of two styles of gameplay loops (Figure 3.18):

- A short story that is meant to be a few hours long
- A game meant to be played long-term, but not for extended periods at a time

From a story perspective, a reason for games to be stressful as pointed out by people is the amount of commitment required to beat a game. Traditional action games can have at minimum 8–10 hours of content; in the 1990s and early 2000s, having 60+ hours was considered the norm for many RPGs. When we add in live service games that are continually updated with new content, there is no end to playing them. Having a shortened game length means that it is possible for someone to get through a game either within one sitting or over a weekend; no long-term commitment to playing the game required. For story-driven games, where the entire reason for playing is following the story, they tend to be on the shorter

Figure 3.18

There is a difference between being designed around a short experience and being able to play a game for one. With something like *Animal Crossing* (left) and other long-form games, someone can put as much or as little time as they want each day when playing it, but the games are meant to be enjoyed for a long time. For something like *A Short Hike* (right), the game was designed so that it could be finished relatively quickly, but there are additional activities if the player chooses to do them that would extend the playtime.

side as it's not possible to stretch out a story's length without hurting the quality of the material.

From a pacing standpoint, designing a shorter game means that there is less time and energy needed to develop and produce content. We can also see this trend in the form of short horror games that became popular in the mid-2010s. Many of which were only between 20 and 30 minutes long and were akin to watching a horror show like "Tales from the Crypt."

Story-driven games are also a plus for writers who are interested in telling a story but may not want to focus on heavy gameplay-related elements. While the bar has been raised thanks to the quality of short-form games, each year we see impressive story-driven games being released that may only take a few hours, or just 30 minutes, to play.

For the second group, this is where games like *The Sims, Stardew Valley*, and *Animal Crossing* fit. Instead of having a fixed completion time, they are meant to be played as much or as little as the player wants. For some people, they may spend hours at a time building the perfect house, playing mini-games, and trying to see as much as possible. Conversely, someone could load the game up, do a few tasks, see what's going on, and then quit and return tomorrow. The same goes for sandbox modes in games like *Minecraft*. For *Animal Crossing*, since the game's calendar is tied to the real world, it provided a structure and reward for consistent playing as opposed to lengthy plays. As a quick tangent, this kind of incentive to turn a game into a daily task would be heavily adopted by the free-to-play and mobile market in the 2010s and can be abused in the sense of conditioning someone to have to play a game every day.

Another key point about the appeal of these games is the use of personalization (Figure 3.19). The terms personalization and customization are often used interchangeably, but there is a specific difference between the two:

Customization – Choices the player can make that affect their ability and options while playing

Personalization – Choices the player can make that affect the look of different characters to go with their referred style

While *Stardew Valley* does have customization with being able to select different perks while leveling up the jobs, it is also known for the level of personalization the player can go after. Their character's clothing and hairstyle can be changed, as well as finding new hats and clothing in the world. Numerous decorations can be bought and placed throughout the farm and their house. Every animal on the farm can be named, and constructed buildings can also be painted to the player's preference.

Personalization, large and small, has been used in all kinds of games. Many live service games will sell personalization options for money; games that have modding support will often get cosmetic mods to give players more ways of affecting the appearance of their characters. Personalization gives someone the ability to

Figure 3.19

Personalization has been a draw in any games that feature multiplayer or a way to share a creation. One of the first goals in any survival crafter is to build the player's living area, which can then be personalized however they want. Games like *Subnautica* (left) allow the player to set up multiple bases in the world. For games where the player is completely free to sculpt the world and the environment as they see fit, they can get very creative as with the many examples in *Minecraft*.

make their characters uniquely theirs and having that kind of space to be creative can be a healthy outlet to de-stress. This is also why many survival crafters have the aforementioned "sandbox" or "creative" mode, so that someone can enjoy the building side of the experience without worrying about losing.

Part of the success and far-reaching appeal of *Animal Crossing New Horizons* was thanks to people posting pictures of their personalized spaces on social media and inviting their friends to visit. This also brings up community engagement as another positive for cozy games. The ability to share characters, homes, farms, and more with other people becomes another way of connecting. With *Stardew Valley* and many crafting games, communities come together to create guides or wikis to help players out. For multiplayer-driven games, the experience becomes even better by being able to play with your friends and directly support each other. With *Stardew Valley*, there were already people building multiplayer mods for it long before that feature was formally added to the game.

When we looked at the rise of the MMOG genre of the 2000s, while plenty of these games featured combat and high-stress situations, they were also known for being able to just immerse the player in the world. Part of the appeal of IP-driven MMOGs was the entire tagline of being a character in their favorite property. The ability to have player/guild-owned homes allowed players to have a place to call

Figure 3.20

And here's my lovely home in *Stardew Valley* filled with the many things I've collected, my wife, and my legendary fish collection.

their own. While the genre has declined dramatically since its peak, this kind of ownership and community has become a part of the cozy/wholesome genres.

Having a space where someone can do what they want free from any comments or criticisms is healthy, and video games for years have been an easy way to have access to personal space. Personalization, again, is about having the freedom to create something uniquely yours; maybe you want to share it with the world, or you can just keep it for yourself (Figure 3.20). Video games can mean many things, and there is nothing wrong with wanting to play highly difficult games to challenge yourself or come home after working and tend a virtual garden with your friends.

People can engage with a game at different levels, which is why games can attract a diverse audience. While not every game can be designed around a wide market, approachability is a big part of growing as a designer, and Chapter 4 is going to focus on it.

3.6 The Limits of Cozy and Wholesome

While cozy and wholesome games are growing in popularity, it's important to stress the limitations of the genre and market in both design and audience. When we look at niche or subgenres in the game industry, the expectations of the fans become more specified. On one hand, it makes it easier to know what you should be putting in your game, but on the other hand, it becomes harder to reach a larger market who prefer or expect more out of a game (Figure 3.21).

Figure 3.21

Stardew Valley's success goes without saying, but it's also important to understand that it is not a perfect game. These Steam achievements are the first ones someone will earn, and already, at least 30% of the people who bought it on Steam stopped playing. This phenomenon will be discussed more in the next chapter.

A platformer, for instance, can be designed around different audiences – casual fans, hardcore ones, etc. With cozy and wholesome, the people who are interested in these games are looking for a particular experience, and if you promote your game as one and fail to deliver, you can risk angering them.

A popular format of horror games that sprung up during the late 2010s are surprise twist games – where things start out being wholesome or cozy…until they're not. The garden the player is growing is really a graveyard full of zombies; the relaxing shop turns out to be the latest murder spree by an axe-wielding maniac, and so on. Even games without the twist but feature dark or disturbing elements out of nowhere can also ruin the vibe of being wholesome. You can still have a game that's cozy with a dark edge to it, but you need to be mindful of what that means to the character and to the person playing it.

As a word of warning, if you are marketing your game as cozy, and it has a horrific twist that comes out of nowhere, it can be upsetting to an audience expecting a peaceful game. While this section has focused more on the vibe of your game, the mechanical aspects of making a cozy and wholesome game will be looked at in Chapter 5.

With *Wanderstop*, the story focuses on a character who is having panic attacks following a traumatic event and trying to rebuild her life. Said panic attacks are shown as dark moments and are there to clash with the cozy elements of the story and the running of the tea shop. However, they are not there as a means of raising the stakes or abruptly adding in a jump scare – their purpose is to show that the character is hurting and that by running the shop (aka, playing the game) she will be able to recover and find peace. If the game just decided to randomly interject the cozy vibes with danger and jump scares, then it wouldn't be a cozy experience.

Adding more to something also doesn't make it inherently better. Another common design strategy seen by developers is to take a popular game or genre and add even more layers of complexity and depth to it. Returning to platformers, the conclusion of this idea was the rage-styled games that have developed their own culture and market over the 2010s. Even with idle design and the evolution of incremental games, there is a fine line between adding depth to give a game more value and adding complexity that makes it harder to get into. At some point, you can add so much to a game that the whole appeal of it in the first place is gone.

With the Bullet Heaven subgenre that blew up thanks to *Vampire Survivors* (released in 2022 by Poncle), there have been many attempts at recreating the success, but they end up with a game that is harder and slower to play. If your game is less enjoyable than the most popular take in a genre, why should someone play it (Figure 3.22)?

If the only idea that you have is to take *Stardew Valley* and add so much that it becomes hard to learn, you may find a market who like that, but you're also going to lose so many of the people who fell in love with *Stardew* in the first place. And

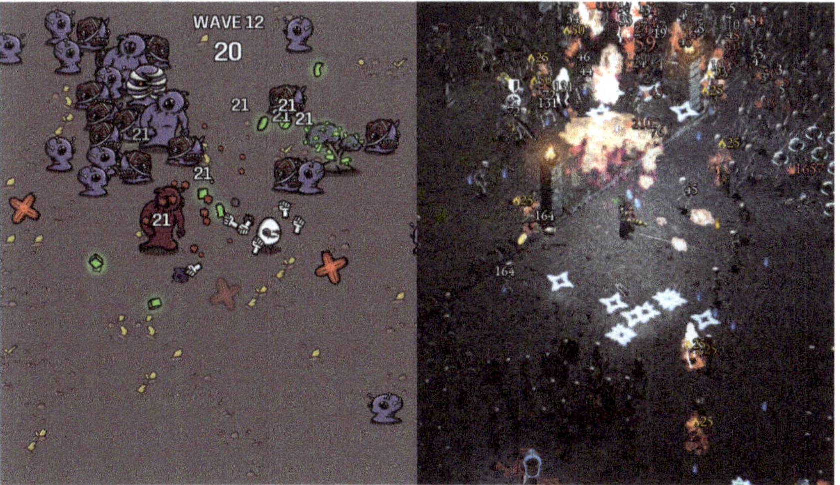

Figure 3.22

Speaking of bullet heavens, two of the most popular ones behind *Vampire Survivors* at the time of writing this are *Brotato* (released in 2023 by Blobfish) and *Halls of Torment* (released in 2024 by Chasing Carrots). Both games stood out by not offering something the same or completely different but taking the base gameplay in a new direction. You can play *Brotato*, *Halls of Torment*, and *Vampire Survivors*, and you won't feel that you're just playing the same game three times.

if your attempt at making a game like *Stardew* is just a worst version of it with nothing new added, no one is going to want to play it.

And remember this lesson, when you combine genres, you are not making a game for fans of genre A and B, but fans specifically looking for genre A + B. Even then, you can run into situations where these mechanics clash with one another; making a 50/50 split all but impossible to achieve.

Many people find peace and relaxation with different games. For action fans like me, I can relax when I'm playing a challenging game that I'm so versed in the rules and systems that I can enter a flow state. However, most people would not find playing a game like *Doom* relaxing or consider it as an example of a cozy game.

A debate that often pops up when discussing wholesome games that's important to avoid is having moral superiority with them. There are fans and creators who have expressed on social media in the past that wholesome games are innately "better" than violent games, or that a wholesome game matters where other games are considered "lesser." An important aspect of growing your knowledge and skill in game design is understanding what attracts and repels people from any genre. While there is an audience for cozy and wholesome games, I wouldn't say they're innately better or worse compared to violent games and vice versa. Thinking about games this way will make it harder to study them and lead to opinions that a game must only be made in one specific way.

The popularity of cozy and wholesome games continues to grow, but if you're expecting your game to make the same amount of sales as *Stardew Valley*, that is probably not going to happen. A common point that comes up with these *Deep Dives* is that there is a difference between the audience for a genre, and the audience for a specific game. Just because *Stardew Valley* sold over 40 million copies, does not mean that there are over 40 million fans of everything cozy/wholesome. Even if you do everything right, that doesn't automatically equate to massive success.

There are a lot of factors that go into every game's success, and just as the bar has grown for reflex-intensive games, so has it for cozy and wholesome. Just making a simple farming title, or short story, is not going to be enough if you want people to take interest in your game. You need to understand how someone plays a game, and for that, it's time to talk about how UI/UX factors into all of this.

Note

1 https://steamspy.com/app/413150

4

Understanding UI/UX Design

4.1 What Is UI/UX Design?

In every *Deep Dive* I've written over the last few years, I've been putting together the same section on UI/UX, but this will be the first book that I'm dedicating an entire chapter to it. If you have read previous *Deep Dives*, you can skip this opening section and go straight to the next one.

The UI represents how someone physically interacts with your game and is often paired with the graphical user interface (**GUI**), which is the on-screen elements that someone will use to play the game. The UX is the feel or aesthetic of your game you are trying to convey. Both are essential to building any video game, not just cozy ones, and the best designers will learn this as early into their career as possible.

When you are thinking about the UI, this is about figuring out the control scheme for your game. Since cozy/casual is not an action-heavy genre, I can't tell you how to perfectly design one, as you must look at the respective genre you are building your game on, and I'll be talking more about the UX in the next section (Figure 4.1).

UI design does have some universal tips that you can use. You need to establish what your default peripheral is that you will be focusing on, with the two most popular being keyboard and mouse or a gamepad. When looking at the peripheral itself, there are two kinds of actions that you will be implementing – primary and

DOI: 10.1201/9781003646860-4

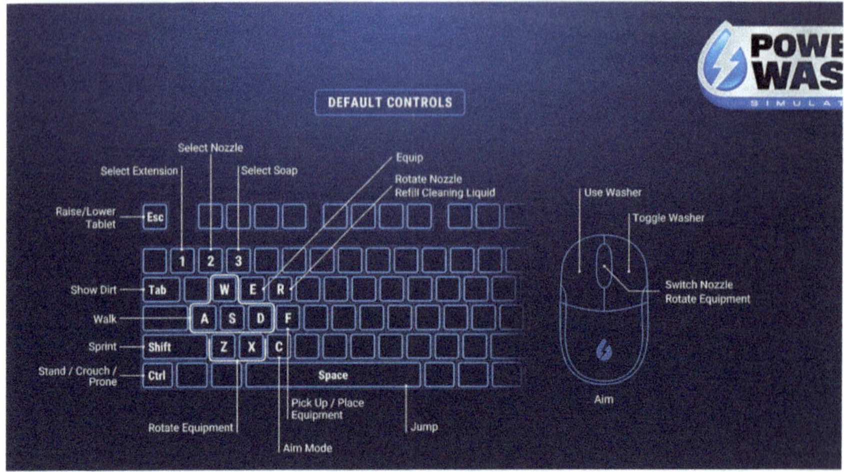

Figure 4.1

This is the default control scheme for *PowerWash Simulator*, and it mirrors the ones used for many shooters, for the obvious reason that the game was built from the framework of a first-person shooter. The controls/the UI is the one place you do want to look at other games to see what people like and don't like in the genre.

secondary. Primary actions are the main verbs that someone will be using every second of play – moving, jumping, shooting, anything that is a part of the core gameplay loop. Secondary actions are context sensitive, which means they will only happen in specific situations: opening a door, pulling a lever, talking to another character. Primary actions should always be assigned to their own keys or buttons, while secondary actions can be tied to the same one and activated within the specific context. An aspect of how UI design has evolved over the years was moving away from each action having its own separate key, but instead, assigning secondary actions to a universal "use" key or button.

The GUI of a game is all about providing the player with all relevant information they need to play it, and this will obviously differ from game to game. The "main screen" is what the player is going to be viewing the most. Your goal is to provide the player with as much view of the game itself while still giving them information. The more elements you have on screen, the harder it will be for someone to focus on the act of playing the game. For cozy/wholesome games, since these games are often less demanding in their gameplay, they will have only a few GUI elements on the screen at a time compared to action-driven titles.

Many designers prefer a "framing" effect for their GUI elements – having them on the corners or edges of the screen so that the main screen is kept uncluttered (Figure 4.2). Another important concept to understand with GUI design is dynamic elements – these are pieces of your GUI that update in real time based on what the player is doing and/or what the mouse pointer is currently on. For games about building structures, if there are conditionals to where buildings can be

Figure 4.2

Looking at this screen from *Stardew Valley*, the yellow lines show how the GUI elements are creating a frame around the top and right sections of the screen. The rectangle in the bottom-left is for any status information to be displayed. Missing from this screenshot is that all buffs on the player will show up on the upper-right. All this creates a framing effect that keeps the main view uncluttered. As another point, notice in this screenshot that the tool GUI is on the top of the screen where it has been previously shown at the bottom. The reason is that the player's character is in the bottom half of the screen and would need to see more down there while doing things. This is an example of a dynamic GUI panel and is important to consider when the need comes up.

placed, or they receive bonuses for being next to other buildings, the GUI should dynamically show if the structure is going to receive a bonus or not.

An underrated example of dynamic GUI design is moving GUI elements in relation to what the player is doing. If there are GUI elements on the top of the screen, when the player is moving up or the camera is focused up there, some games will shift the GUI elements to the bottom of the screen so that the player can see more of what's going on without the GUI blocking them.

The goal of your GUI is to give the player any and all the information that will be required to play the game; if the player needs to leave the game to consult a guide or wiki to understand a fundamental part of your gameplay, then something is wrong with your UI/UX.

A key part of UI/UX design is understanding approachability vs. accessibility features and how they relate to the experience of your game. Accessibility features help someone play a game if they have an outside condition preventing them – colorblind mode, subtitles, compatibility with specific controllers, and many more. There are special interest groups (SIGs) and organizations like the International Game Developers Association Game Accessibility SIG: https://igda-gasig.org/ and AbleGamers respectively who have compiled information and methodology around accessibility.

Approachability features are those that make a game easier to play and improve the playability of it. Many approachability features are referred to as quality of life, as they're not changing the game itself, but making it easier to play. To create a list of every approachability feature one could use is impossible, as there are designers who come up with new ways of experiencing popular genres each year.

What you need to understand is that every approachability feature is an accessible one, but not every accessibility option makes your game more approachable. This is part of UI/UX design and understanding what it means to play your game and how someone plays your game. Having all the accessibility features in the world will not help your game if it's horrible to play. Likewise, not thinking about accessibility can make your game unplayable for potential customers. This also means not purposely adding in elements that can negatively affect people, such as flashing lights or strobe effects.

In today's market, whether you are a single developer or part of a huge company, you cannot ignore UI/UX. When I talk about how fast someone can stop playing a game, UI/UX problems are often the first reason, which have led to countless games churning players within 10 minutes of starting it up (Figure 4.3).

Figure 4.3

Game feel is a very hard concept to describe to the uninitiated, but games without good feel are often the ones that don't retain their players. Conversely, if it feels great to just move around, jump, swing a sword, etc., players are more willing to put up with challenging gameplay. There's a difference between being challenged by a section that expects the player to be skilled and being challenged because the game doesn't control right and the player is fighting it to proceed. The games shown here have their own specific feel to them that is required if someone has any intent on finishing them (games shown are *Hollow Knight* and *Elden Ring*).

This entire chapter represents some of the easiest ways to ruin your game, and as someone who has been covering indie games for more than a decade at the time of writing this, I have seen and experienced just about every UI/UX mistake one could imagine. I'll be repeating this piece of advice throughout the rest of the book, but the best way to study UI/UX is to play a lot of games of your chosen genre – all the good ones, all the bad ones, and everything in-between. If there's something you really like, take note of it; conversely, if something annoys or frustrates you, also note it. This is what becomes a part of your UX that I will be focusing on next.

Surprisingly, I've seen UI/UX issues come from developers who already have a background in development almost as much as first timers. The reason is that you can't learn UI/UX by just watching game footage, you need to experience the game to see how it feels in your hands. From hardcore action-driven games to slow-paced menu-driven ones; the only way you'll be able to study them effectively is to be the one playing them. The earlier in your career that you learn UI/UX, the better your games will be because of it.

4.2 Defining the User Experience

The UX, as I said in the previous section, is the feel of your game mechanics that you are trying to convey, but what does that mean exactly? When we examine the UI of a game, we can look at easily defined elements – what is your control scheme, what GUI elements are someone looking at? But the UX is something that forms based on your design and UI. You can have an idea of what kind of UX you want for your game, but it is created by the total of your entire gameplay.

Do you want the player to feel sad, happy, in control, confused, or any other emotion (Figure 4.4)? When I study a game's design, what I'm looking for is determining what UX the developer wanted for their game and did it succeed or fail. While this may sound difficult, once you start studying designs and playing a variety of games, you can start to deduce this.

Part of the UX is also defining the specific market for your game, and again, this is not just for cozy/wholesome games, but any game ever made. If a designer wants to create a high-octane action game with guns, explosions, and the player is supposed to feel like an unstoppable killing machine, and the entire game starts out with an hour of slow-paced sneaking missions, that is a conflict with the UX.

With the entire idea of cozy and wholesome games vs. other designs, let's pose two kinds of experiences using the same mechanics about deep sea diving in first person:

- Game A: A first-person horror game where players must dive to find scavenged weapons needed to kill a giant monster that is stalking their every move while making sure they don't run out of oxygen and drown.

Figure 4.4

The UX represents the "tone" or "mood" of your game. While you may not be thinking about it from the moment you start designing your game, your decisions and gameplay will determine your experience. Sometimes, you can have aesthetics that match, even if they might clash a bit, such as people pairing Isabelle with the Doom Slayer.

- Game B: A first-person exploration game where the player is taking an undersea tour of a peaceful cove, diving to take snapshots of all the different aquatic animals and collect coral that they can fashion into jewelry to wear or sell to people on the surface. Oxygen tanks provide infinite air, and there are no predators in the water.

Both games make use of similar systems and are played in first-person. However, the experience of playing them is wildly different, and if you try to market either game to the wrong audience, you're going to end up with a failure.

Growing as a designer is being able to think about your UX and how your mechanics and systems can facilitate that experience for the consumer. This will aid you in all parts of design, as knowing who your market is will allow you to focus better on gameplay that appeals to them. Your goal when it comes to the UX is making a game that is enjoyable for your core market but still provides a means for other people to be able to experience it.

Some may misconstrue that into trying to make the "every game" – a game that appeals to everyone in the entire world, but the truth is that there is no such thing as the game that appeals to everyone. What you want is to hit your core demographic but also provide a way for someone who is interested, but is not a superfan, to try and learn it. This goes along with playtesting and getting a wide spectrum of people to look at your game that I will talk about in the next section. A great game has a core audience – the people who the gameplay is directly for, but there is also the group who are interested in trying out something that is being heavily praised. They might not know who the designer is, or have played games of this type before, but this is the chance to possibly win over a new audience.

If your game is not approachable, that does not mean you have a bad game. There are plenty of amazing and original games that are so niche you will never hear about them unless you already belong to those social circles. What it means is that your game will not easily break out into the larger market. For some developers, that's not a problem, because they are already budgeting their game modestly and know that it's not going to be the next billion-dollar success (Figure 4.5). To that last point, understanding the potential reach of your game is another important step in growing as a designer. I've seen games with incredibly hardcore fans who absolutely love to play it, but looking at the completion rates, more than 80% of the consumer base stopped within 20 minutes. If your experience is being marketed toward a niche audience, and you budget it accordingly, you can still succeed. However, no matter how loudly your fans yell about how great your game is, it's important to be aware and budget your game accordingly for a smaller market.

Conversely, there is also the risk that the more you water down the core gameplay loop, you can alienate your fans who are looking for a specific experience.

Figure 4.5

Here we have two very different games: *Geneforge 2 – Infestation* by Spiderweb Software and *Old Skies* by Wadjet Eye Games. Both titles come from veterans in their respective genres, and they both understand the reach of their designs and the relative size of their markets. Surviving as an indie developer at this level, even having popular games, is about knowing what to focus your time and budget on to create an experience that your fans are looking for.

Niche genres like grand strategy, puzzle, and adventure games all have unique qualifiers that distinguish them from the rest of the market. Part of the growing pains of the adventure genre has been trying to square the circle of bringing in new fans who aren't used to grueling puzzles or having to search for the correct pixels from the classics of the genre, while still providing something entertaining for the fans who have grown up with the genre for decades. Puzzle games have evolved into presenting them as a massive world of puzzles rather than just dozens of individualized levels, and there have been several amazing puzzle games that have gotten critical success in the space, such as *Lorelei and the Laser Eyes* and *Blue Prince* (released in 2024 and 2025 by Simogo and Dogubomb respectively). Unfortunately, I can't give you an easy answer to this – anything you add or remove from your game will affect the audience for it, but you need to decide what your game is going to be.

A constant struggle for new developers is not settling on a UX and frequently changing it at the whims of other people or because another idea popped into their heads. When you change your UX, much like your core gameplay loop, you are, in essence, building a new game. It's not so bad if you're only a few weeks into a project; it's another matter entirely if you are months or years in.

With reaching a wider audience, you will run into people who like the idea of your game, but they don't like the core gameplay loop. If you're building a game detailing the struggles of living with a debilitating disease, someone suggesting a game mode that removes all those limitations would ruin the message of the game.

However, if you're building an action game and there is a sizable audience looking for an easier, or harder version of it, you may want to consider having different difficulty settings to allow the player to fine-tune their experience.

This is one of the reasons why you need to playtest your game and understand what it means to set your UX. As the designer, you need to know when to bend and when to hold when it comes to the intended experience. Returning to the disease example, if you want more people to experience just the story of your game, then turning off those features would give more people a chance to see it. With the difficulty example, if you are only focusing on a challenging experience, and targeting that specific market, whether by intent or by limitations in your budget, then it may not be worth it to pursue difficulty settings. And there's nothing stopping you from adding in new modes and content after a game is released to reach a new market, however, you must be careful with how you budget continued work on a game after it is released.

What you must do is balance the experience you are trying to make with the resources at your disposal. A major trend that is going through the game industry in the 2020s is looking at being sustainable in the industry. For companies today, it's no longer about trying to only make that one dream game but being able to survive as a studio after each game. Defining and sticking to your UX will enable you to think about your game's reach, and conversely, what you should put into it.

A poignant discussion about this was an interview with designer Xalavier Nelson from Strange Scaffold about making the short-form game *Clickolding* (released in 2024) (Figure 4.6). In it, he described funding the game as such:

> If you make a game faster or more cheaply, you can justify its existence far more easily. There's a version of *Clickolding* that costs $500,000. That game doesn't exist. The version of *Clickolding* that does exist costs $25,000.[1]
>
> **– Xalavier Nelson, Wired Interview**

Your UX, next to the core gameplay loop, is going to be the throughlines of your entire game. When you are trying to figure out what to add next, you need to be referencing both.

With defining the differences between cozy, wholesome, and casual, these are very specific UX that I will be focusing on in the next chapter, and while not every genre is as specific, you cannot ignore this part of your design, especially in today's market.

To wrap up this section: How does the UX mesh with your game design? This goes with the market for your game and what you should be thinking about is once again the emotion that you want someone to be feeling. If you are setting out to make a very challenging game, what does that mean to someone who is a fan? What about an entry-level example?

Figure 4.6

Strange Scaffold has been an up and coming studio for the past few years while drafting this book. Each one of their games is completely different and aimed at a different audience but still has the same vibe and style. The aesthetic of your studio can often be as important as having one for your games, with New Blood Interactive being another popular example among indie fans (games shown – top left: *Space Warlord Organ Trading Simulator*, top right: *El Paso Elsewhere*, bottom left: *Clickolding*, bottom right: *I Am Your Beast*).

Some of my favorite games I've seen over the 2010s–2020s are those that purposely target consumers who aren't the hardcore fans of a genre and instead try to make something that works as a gateway to that design. One of the most successful games was *Balatro* by LocalThunk, released in 2024, and the design was to use poker rules and mechanics as a gateway toward learning deckbuilding design. It is extremely easy to grasp the basics, but mastering the game is an entirely different story. To that point, what often separates the massive successes from niche ones is being able to easily present their mechanics and systems to newcomers and veterans alike.

The games that go on to be big successes are thanks to having a great UI/UX and not despite it. This is often the difference between a good game that succeeds among only its fanbase versus a game that blows up and becomes known all throughout the industry and market. And to understand what consumers want, it's time to talk about playtesting.

4.3 Playtesting Practices

Given all the *Deep Dives* I've written up to this point, it is finally time to discuss playtesting and why it is a required part of making a successful game.

Playtesting is about allowing someone to test your game during development and use their feedback to make changes going forward. That last sentence may seem very simple, but playtesting is a vital part of the development process and has often been part of the reason for games failing. This is a part of the development process that isn't often talked about or taught, but it is one you need to know about.

Playtesting can occur at various points of a game's development. Many designers will show proof of concept builds of their games to trusted friends and family. These builds are often quite literally the very first playable prototype for that game. There may not be any art assets created, and it is the roughest state of a game. The goal is to see if people respond to this specific gameplay – if you can make a game that has no created art, just all placeholder images, engaging to play, then you are onto something. Part of the appeal of game jams has been creating prototypes of game concepts, and there have been many successful games that all started as nothing more than an entry in a jam.

From that point, it is up to the designer's discretion as to when they will do playtesting and on what features. Playtesting can have different purposes depending on the game and how far into development it is. Some developers may get playtesters to look at a specific part of the game, such as having a multiplayer playtest session to see how the game handles with a group playing. Many studios have used playtesting as an incentive for preordering a game or to reward their most hardened fans with something exclusive. A major opportunity for developers today who are on Steam is to use the Steam Early Access program for their games (Figure 4.7). Early access acts as a way of buying a game that's still in development, allowing consumers to offer advice and help guide the rest of the development until its release.

Figure 4.7

Playtesting is important for all games, but its role has expanded over the years with the use of Steam Early Access. For games like *Duskers* (left) and *The Rogue Prince of Persia* (right), where there is the added challenge of procedural generation, it's not possible for a small team to be able to check every possible permutation. With *Slime Rancher 2* (center), playtesting and early access allow designers to see what the community thinks of any new changes or additions and continue to expand accordingly.

However, you must understand that using early access as playtesting is different from hiring dedicated playtesters. When a game is released on early access, that game is essentially out and available for purchase. Many indie developers make the mistake of treating their early access as a means of getting an influx of cash to then continue working on their game. By the time your game is ready for early access, it must be at the point that you are comfortable with selling it to consumers, and that also means having people playtest it prior.

What you are looking for when playtesting are the following:

- Are playtesters enjoying my game?
- Do they understand how to play it?
- Are they struggling with any aspect of the gameplay?
- What do they like about the game?
- What do they dislike about the game?
- Specific details about your design

Good playtesting is not about sending out game keys to the ether and hoping that someone sends you an email back. With your early rounds of playtesting, you want to be actively reaching out to people that you trust – other designers, fans of your previous games, and even local game clubs can work in this capacity.

You want to come prepared with questions to ask the playtesters about the overall game and anything specific to the experience. If you are interested in a specific part of your design, make sure to have a question about it, and if possible, give the playtesters a build that focuses on it. One of the best ways to get useful information through playtesting is to record the person, ideally with you not watching them at the time. If you know the tester has recording software, ask them if they can record their session. Pay attention to any spots where the person is having trouble making progress or outright gets stuck in your game. If there is a common area or concern by playtesters, that should be the next thing you focus on.

While you can trust people you know, there will always come a time while playtesting that you must expand to newcomers. Hardcore fans are great at articulating what they want out of an experience or genre, but they are not the best when trying to see what it's like to play your game from a fresh perspective (Figure 4.8). The new player's experience is a do-or-die moment for many games – if your title is frustrating to play, or the player is confused at the start, they are not going to stick around. It is common to cycle through playtesters, because once someone has already playtested your game, they will not be able to give you a new player's perspective on it for a future build.

Figure 4.8

Games can change dramatically during their development, and with early access, gamers can see how the scope and design can be altered. Best-case scenario, the game is going to become better with each new update. Worst-case scenario, a game's development can feel like two steps forward, three steps back. The games shown here have all gone through early access and grew and changed by the feedback from the player base, and why you will always need fresh eyes to see how these changes feel to a new player (games shown: A: *Hades 2*, B: *Don't Starve*, C: *Cook Serve Forever*, D: *Beyond Sunset*).

For hardcore fans, they are more willing to put up with pain points of either your design specifically, or the ones inherent in the genre. There are more examples that I can count of consumers offering advice to designers on forums only to have them being shouted out by the hardcore fans. With your UX, you must decide who you are trying to reach. Designing a game that only appeals to 100 people is not going to sustain you as a studio, no matter how vocal they are about what they want.

The nightmare about player feedback and why providing you with an easy-to-follow guide for playtesting is impossible is that everyone is different, even from the same consumer base. You can have ten different people give you ten different complaints or praises about your game, and yet they're all talking about the same thing. It's up to you to decipher feedback, and it is again why having as large of a pool of playtesters that you can find is vital. To prove this point, here's an example of feedback you could get while building an action game:

- I keep dying, this game is terrible
- The first boss is impossible
- Why can't I hit anything?
- The enemies are horrible to fight
- Your game sucks
- This game is too easy and boring

Unless you are hiring someone knowledgeable on quality assurance or QA, you are not going to be getting detailed feedback from your playtesters. Some people will just leave a negative comment and that will be the end of it. With these points about the game being frustrating to play and players having a hard time fighting, we could hypothesize that something is not right about the general combat mechanics. With the last comment, you will have hardcore fans who want your game to be as difficult as possible and are more than happy hitting their head against the metaphorical brick wall, but you once again need to ask yourself if that's the UX you are targeting.

Some developers take playtesting to mean that they should only listen to positive responses:

- I love your game
- Your game is perfect
- Don't change anything
- This is the best game I've ever played

But that leads to developers only listening to an echo chamber of praise from their hardcore fans and friends. There are countless stories of developers being blindsided when they put their game in front of someone at a convention or when watching a first-timer play it and see that they absolutely are not getting it.

Remember, it is rarely the consumer's fault if they aren't figuring out your game. There are rare cases of someone who is just not the right audience for a game – someone who hates being scared and they decide to try a horror game. More often than not, however, if someone cannot figure out the basics of your game through onboarding, then that is a failure by you.

Earlier in this section, I brought up Steam Early Access as a pseudo-form of playtesting, and while developers have used it as such, succeeding on it requires a different approach to community engagement and content updates that is different from what we're discussing here.

Part of the problem with effective playtesting is that many developers are often limited by their reach and notoriety. If a famous designer like Hideo Kojima of *Metal Gear Solid* and *Death Stranding* fame puts out the word that he's looking for playtesters, he will get thousands of signups immediately. For a first-time developer or student project, you may be lucky to get five. This is the point where playtesting and marketing coincide, as part of your marketing for any game is figuring out who and where the audience for it is. There is always a forum/discord/messaging board of fans out there. Depending on where you live, there may be local game clubs or colleges with game design courses with people happy to check out something new.

Not everyone is going to have access to playtesting, and that means for some of you reading this, your only feedback is going to come after the game is released. Besides iterating on a game's design during development, you should also be looking at improvements from game to game (Figure 4.9). Another design trap I've seen is when someone just keeps remaking the same game: Instead of fighting green monsters with a yellow sky, they're fighting yellow monsters with a green sky. While marketing problems are often one of the main reasons for a game failing, it's important to look at the response from the people who played your game and see how they fared with it.

For games built around live-service design – that will receive frequent content updates – playtesting is even more important. Every new gameplay addition to your game will affect the current state of it. Not having any playtesting done can lead to unintentional bugs showing up, or even worse, the new features making the game unplayable for any number of reasons. Consumers are only willing to up with issues like this for so long before they get fed up and stop playing your game. At this stage of your game's lifespan, you should have a dedicated QA department whose job it is to go through any new content that's to be added.

The entire goal of this section is to make you understand how important it is to iterate and grow as a designer. The consumer will only give you so much leeway with problems in your game before they move on and never return. Being able to understand how someone responds to your game will make you a better designer, and the earlier in your career that you learn how to do proper playtesting, the faster you will be able to grow your skills.

Figure 4.9

Everyone wants their first game to be a huge success like *Balatro* here, but there's a difference between your first created project and your first released game. Just because the first game that you know about from a developer is a success doesn't mean that this idea came from nowhere. There can be dozens of failed prototypes, unfinished projects, or games that never earned a single sale, before someone has that great idea. This is why you need to be able to finish your projects when you can and learn from those experiences.

4.4 The Causes of Churn

The goal of studying UI/UX is to reduce the churn rate of your game. Churn, for our purposes, is the percentage of players who leave your game negatively and cannot be counted on as future consumers for your subsequent games.

Churn can happen for any number of reasons, even something as basic as someone not liking your GUI when they start playing. Every game that has and will exist in the future will have churn to it (Figure 4.10). As I said earlier, there is no such thing as the perfect video game, and to this day, there hasn't been a game where 100% of the people who bought it were able to finish it. Your purpose when studying and implementing UI/UX practices is to keep people interested in playing your game for as long as possible, and that when they decide to stop playing it, they do so without hating your game.

Most churn will spike within the first 5 to 10 minutes of playing a game; this is why the new player's experience is so crucial. What happens every time is that the churn rates will stabilize; they will still go down, but at a smaller rate and will look something like this with your achievement rates:

- 100%
- 65%

Figure 4.10

Two of the biggest games released in 2025 are *Clair Obscur: Expedition 33* (by Sandfall Interactive) and *Hollow Knight: Silksong* (by Team Cherry). While both are being highly praised, they are still subject to people not enjoying them and quitting within the first few minutes, which is again why I say that there is no such thing as the universally loved game.

- 63%
- 45%
- 43%
- 42.5%
- 40.7% and so on

The worst possible outcome is a massive loss of your player base within minutes of starting your game – losing 80% or more of the player base within 20 minutes of playing, and no, that is not hyperbole, there are games out there where that has happened.

With the points about sustainability raised so far, not understanding the size of your potential consumer base has been the underlying killer of many small to mid-sized studios in the 2010s. For myself, I have studied the achievement rates and UI/UX of just about every game I've played for more than seven years. Whenever a game frustrates me for any reason, I go to the achievement page to see if there is a huge churn rate spike. As a developer, studying these metrics will give you an estimated idea of your potential fanbase going forward. Just because your game sold 500,000 copies does not mean that everyone is going to come back for your next title. But if you budget your game under the assumption that they will, you can find yourself with a game whose consumer base is not going to be able to justify the budget, and if that keeps happening, you won't have any budget to keep producing games.

Churn is often the silent killer of many game studios who started out with a modest or huge success. The first game, or the first break-out success, from any studio/franchise is never the accurate measurement of your audience. When people hear about a hot new game, they will check it out to see what the buzz is. However, even if they don't end up refunding it, if they stop playing almost immediately, you can guarantee that they are not going to be coming back for your next game (Figure 4.11).

One way to examine the overall success of your game is by using the achievement rates as a means of charting how far people played into your game. Figuring out your fanbase depends on the length of your game and genre, especially looking at the differences between short and long games. If people are stopping 8 hours into a 10-hour game, there is a good chance they're going to be interested in your next game. Conversely, if they are stopping 15 hours into an 80-hour game, more than likely they're not coming back. While you want people to finish your game, there are always factors that can lead to them quitting, which isn't because of frustration. For adults, the simplest reason is that real life gets in the way. Sometimes people leave a game once they've seen all the major points to it and have gotten their fill.

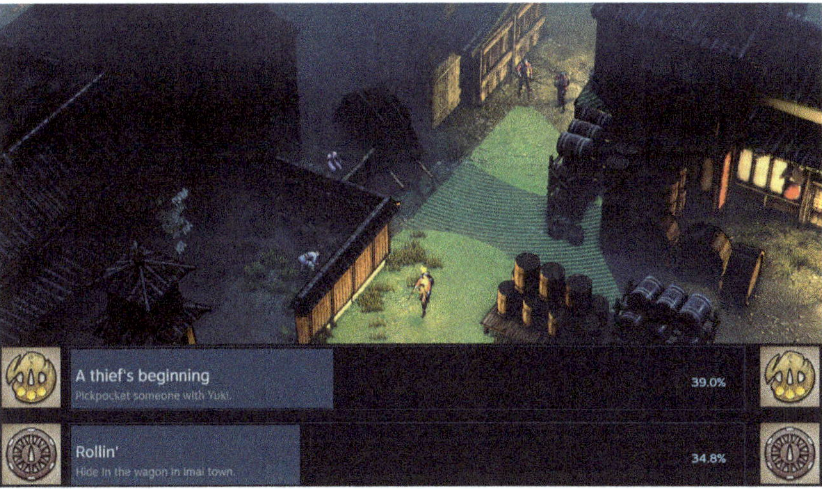

Figure 4.11

This is *Shadow Tactics: Blades of the Shogun* from Mimimi Games (released in 2016). Not only did it become the banner game from the studio, but it also brought back the tactical stealth genre. While it was highly praised, it was very difficult to play and lost more than 60% of its players in less than 90 minutes of play. The achievements shown are the two I got that went along with finishing the first two missions. Their next game *Desperados 3* (released in 2020) was even harder and had high churn. When the studio closed in 2024 after the release of *Shadow Gambit: The Cursed Crew*, they tried to make a more approachable take on the genre, but it was too late to try and attract new fans. It's a harsh reminder that even if a game becomes a critical success, that does not mean it will be a commercial one.

Returning to the previous section, part of what you want out of playtesting is figuring out any pain points in your game, as these are often the biggest sources of churn. Is there a part of your game where you notice a lot of people are quitting? Returning to the point about churn spikes, if most players are quitting around the same time, then it's important to investigate what could be the possible reasons. And if you do discover a major problem, you will have two choices: spend work on the game to fix said problem, or take what you've learned and correct it for your next game. I've seen examples of studios who have done one or the other with specific pros and cons.

By fixing your game, you can use this as a marketing event to get people back into it and hope they spread the word. However, this means investing more money in a game that didn't succeed and hoping that you can turn it around.

Releasing a new game allows you to reach fans and those who didn't enjoy the first one and tell them that the new game is going to be even better. In this respect, it will lead to the previous game becoming obsolete, with consumers wanting to just play the "superior" version of your gameplay.

For games of specific niches, like casual/wholesome, churn rates are a little different. Niche games that appeal to a specific audience will often have lower churn spikes, because the people who are buying these games are the key demographic; they're not going to be surprised or frustrated and end up quitting early. For a game that does break out and reach a larger audience, what can end up happening is that the game has a huge churn spike right in the beginning – thanks to all the new people checking it out from word of mouth and realizing it's not for them. In this case, you can have a churn rate that goes something like this:

- 88%
- 55%
- 53%
- 52.1% and so on

You may be wondering why it doesn't start at 100%, and that's because there are people who will quit a game before they even get to when the game starts, and yes, that is normal to see. There is no agreed-upon standard for what constitutes a good clear rate for any game, with more people always being better. For an average game's length of 8–10 hours, if your game has a clear rate of at least 30–35% of the consumer base, I would consider that to be a modest success.

One final point about studying churn rates is that what I've talked about in this section mostly pertains to indie development. You cannot hold a AAA release to the same metrics and standards, as they have several factors that are unique to them (Figure 4.12):

- There is a sense of prestige in playing the hottest new game that gets more people to check it out

Figure 4.12

For a very odd pairing, this is *Death Stranding 2: On the Beach* and *Donkey Kong Bananza*, the former is from Hideo Kojima and the latter by Nintendo. Both games did not have an ounce of trouble with marketing, and the name and reputation of these studios meant that people were going to find out and be interested in them no matter what. For most of you reading this book, you will unfortunately not have that same level of fame with your game.

- Consumers are more willing to put up with pain points in large, and more expensive games, given the investment required to play them
- The fanbase of a popular studio will often pick up and play a new game from them regardless of the genre
- The marketing budget for these games means that far more people will see and know about them compared to indie games

The next time you finish a game that you loved, or stopped playing because of something you hated, if it's on Steam, check out the achievement rates and see what the consumer base generally thought about it. Once you start understanding the purpose of UI/UX design, it will allow you to further examine games to see what causes these problems and potential solutions for your game.

For a positive note to end this section on, there are many first-time indie developers who are making amazing games without needing years of experience in the game industry, and I've spoken to many of them in my time. The secret is that these designers grew up playing the games they loved, while understanding why someone may hate them or find them frustrating. Once you start studying churn, you will not look at a game the same way ever again.

Earlier in this chapter, I brought up games that did a great job of acting as a gateway for new consumers, and each one of these games, without a shadow of doubt, studied the UI/UX of the genre to understand the exact parts that frustrate new and existing players. How you present information and gameplay to someone is just as important as the mechanics themselves if you expect your game to reach a large audience.

Remember this final point: Your hardcore fans will stick with you through thick and thin and are often the least receptive to pain points, but everyone else will be far more critical. For developers who don't study UI/UX and best practices, putting their game in front of people for the first time can be a humbling moment of seeing what people really think of it. While you can't please everyone, you at least want people to give your game more than a few seconds of play.

4.5 Assessing Approachability and Aesthetics

Everything that is UI/UX related in your game will impact the approachability of it, and there are no defined metrics for approachability in the same way that there are standards for accessibility.

While this does make it difficult to set an agreed-upon definition, in my opinion, approachability can be defined by how easy it is for someone to experience a game. While this begins with your onboarding and any tutorials, it extends to the moment-to-moment gameplay and the core gameplay loop (Figure 4.13).

Just because a tutorial was easy or the player grasped what was going on doesn't mean they are going to be figuring out the actual game. There are countless grand strategy titles known for being demanding and borderline impossible to learn if you're not already a fan of them. Even if someone gets through the tutorial, playing the full game can be a different story. When we bring difficult games to the discussion, approachability becomes even more muddled to grasp.

There are people who feel that any pain points, bad UI/UX elements, and churn causers, are the best parts of playing a game. This brings up the "vocal minority" of many niche genres and franchises who are vehemently against any UI/UX improvements due to the fear of it "dumbing down" the game. Conversely, you can have a game that is designed to be difficult, and hardcore fans are now complaining that it's ***too difficult*** for them. As the designer, you are the final judge as to what the experience of your game is going to look like, and that means drawing a line in the sand for how approachable it is.

Since this is a book about cozy and wholesome games, you need to be extra attentive to how it feels to play your game, and why I dedicated an entire chapter to discussing UI/UX. Even in games that are meant to be relaxing and low stakes, it can still be frustrating and annoying to play if no thought was given to the UI/UX.

To start examining the approachability of your game, you need to start with the core gameplay loop of it – what is the purpose of playing this game? Once that's decided, you need to run every mechanic, system, and GUI element under that lens to see if there are any clashes. An easy way to spot approachability issues is if the player must do something that takes them away from the core gameplay loop. Even if this is only for a few seconds at a time, those seconds will add up over the course of playing.

Figure 4.13

Here's a fun example of how approachability can change the perception and appeal of a game. These three screenshots all belong to tactical strategy games despite each one looking very different from one another. *XCOM 2* (released in 2016 by Firaxis) came out first and was built exclusively for PC and hardcore fans of the series and design, while *Mario + Rabbids* (released in 2017 by Ubisoft Milan and Ubisoft Paris) was designed as a tactical strategy game that could fit on the Nintendo Switch and for newcomers. The approachability not only made it more appealing than *XCOM 2* to try but became a template for developers to make their own versions of tactical strategy, and how we got *Persona 5 Tactica* (released in 2023 by Atlus).

A classic example of this is the repeated use of "menuing" or when the player must leave the main screen to perform tasks through various menus before going back to the main screen. If the player must constantly stop what they're doing and perform this work, it will eventually wear on their nerves.

Approachability issues are some of the biggest points I raise when I see them, because they do not go away – if a part of a game is annoying 20 seconds in, that's going to be there until the game is finished (Figure 4.14). Some people are willing to look past them; others will quit immediately.

If you can do anything that reduces the time the player is not performing the core gameplay loop, the better your game will be for it. Here's a popular example of how a genre became more approachable with that practice. Action role-playing games (ARPGs) are a combination of real-time combat with managing gear, attributes, and other role-playing elements. These games are famous for dumping an avalanche of equipment on the player and asking them to figure out which ones are the best to use while clogging up their inventory screen with dozens of swords, chest pieces, potions, and more. Over the years, designers have been evolving the

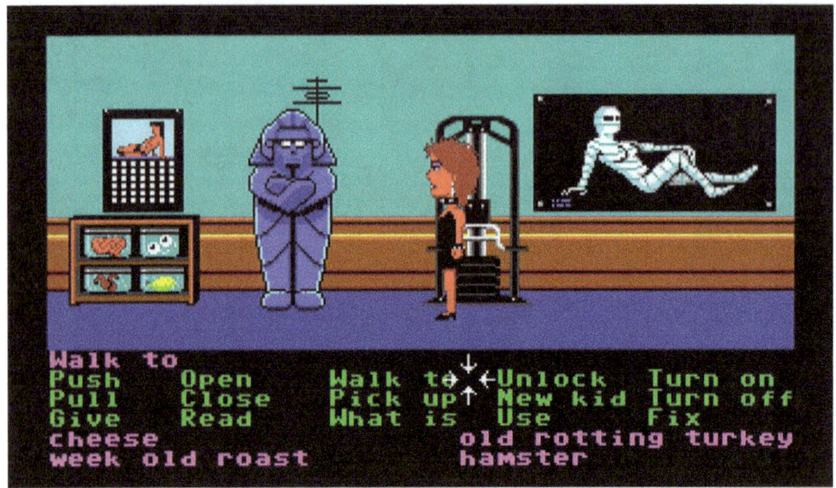

Figure 4.14

Another example of how approachability can lead to evolutions in a genre comes from adventure games. This is a scene from *Maniac Mansion* that was released in 1987 (developed by Lucasfilm Games) as one of the early successes of the adventure genre. Pictured at the bottom is the verb menu, requiring the player to pick the correct verb to go with any interaction in the game. It is clunky to use but was the standard for early adventure games. It wouldn't be until the 1990s when developers streamlined the actions into a few choices that it became easier to play the genre.

GUI and UI/UX when it comes to gear to make this process as efficient as possible with the following improvements:

- Being able to instantly compare the selected gear to what's equipped and see what attributes are different
- Instantly sorting the inventory and automatically combining resource items together
- Setting item filters that will only show relevant gear to the player's build when it drops on the field

With these changes, it opened the genre for more players to enjoy, and at the same time, veteran fans loved these improvements, because without them, it slowed down the game. This is a perfect example of how approachability features can improve how a game plays – the purpose of playing an ARPG is to run around fighting monsters and throwing out special abilities, not standing still for 20 minutes comparing 40 different pants and shirts to figure out which combination is the best.

Another avenue to improve the playability of a game is to have dynamic commands or context-sensitive ones that I touched on at the start of this chapter.

In many crafting-style games, the player will often have to switch between multiple tools used to harvest resources – an axe for cutting down trees, a pickaxe for breaking rocks, and so on. The common practice is to require the player to manually switch between the respective tools each time they want to gather a resource. A streamlined version of this is making the "harvest" command context sensitive – so that the game will automatically equip the required tool (provided the player has it in their inventory) whenever they are trying to harvest a resource.

An interesting approach we've seen is when games of keyboard-heavy genres are ported, or redesigned, for consoles. A gamepad is a fundamentally different peripheral compared to having a keyboard and mouse, which requires a complete redesign of how the genre can work for it. The series *Pikmin* by Nintendo (first released in 2001) was Nintendo's take on the real-time strategy genre (RTS). The RTS genre is notorious for being button-heavy to play, even more so if we're talking about competitive matches. Instead of trying to make *Pikmin* like other RTS games, Nintendo redesigned the experience to work without the need for multiple keys and a mouse pointer. Part of what they did was to remove a lot of the finer control normally associated with RTS games, because there literally weren't enough buttons on a GameCube controller to fit them. Instead, all interactions with the game's environment and enemies were handled by throwing the Pikmin at them, which in turn, they would perform a context-sensitive action related to what they were thrown at. Instead of *Pikmin* trying to chase after the same audience of RTS fans, it created a new fanbase who were looking for something different from the genre.

Being able to redesign how someone plays your game based on the platform they're on can lead to a new audience experiencing something for the first time. When *Diablo 3* by Blizzard Entertainment was released in 2012, the game was designed with a keyboard and mouse UI like all ARPGs that came before it. It surprised fans when Blizzard released the game on consoles starting in 2013, as ARPGs were rarely released due to the limited button inputs on a gamepad. What Blizzard did was rebuild the UI/UX for a gamepad and streamlined most of the commands to fit on it. A major example was providing console players with a "dodge" command to make it easier for them to avoid damage due to an analog stick not providing as precise control compared to a mouse and keyboard. On PC, each class had a "defensive move" that needed to be equipped for players to use it during combat. The console release was a brilliant move, and not only did it give the series a new market, but the UI/UX would be copied by other ARPG designers throughout the decade for both console releases and as an alternative control scheme for PC players.

Another popular approachability feature seen in PC games is the use of "hotkeys." A hotkey is when pressing a key or keys on the keyboard, it will perform a command that normally requires a mouse click. Hotkeys allow someone to control a game faster, and for competitive titles, they become a necessity to outplay their opponents. There is no guideline set for the number of hotkeys or which ones to prioritize in any given genre. The best advice I can give is to examine which actions the players are doing the most and see if there are ways of using hotkeys to speed things up.

The **aesthetics** of your game represent the emotion you are trying to make the player feel and are key when we're talking about cozy/wholesome games. If the core gameplay loop and aesthetic are about running a peaceful bed and breakfast and interacting with all the people who come to stay in it, requiring the player to spend 30 minutes going over itemized lists of all money and resources spent would be an example of a clash. Conversely, if you are trying to make an incredibly detailed simulation of running a bed and breakfast, then ***not*** having that would be a clash here (Figure 4.15).

Consumers want different experiences when they buy a game, and you want to be crystal clear about what the experience of your game is like and make sure that the aesthetics match. This also gets at marketing and promoting your game, which are off-topic for this book. To briefly go over this, you will need to show people through images, trailers, and gifs, what your game is about and the kind of experience they will get out of playing your game. Every genre has YouTubers, journalists, and streamers who will cover it, and part of your job will be to find them and reach out to them about your game.

Figure 4.15

Knowing who your demographic is for your game will affect the decision making that goes into your onboarding and approachability. This is a screenshot from *Business Heroes Street Grub* that is in early access as of writing this book (developed by Visionaries), which I did playtesting for. The game's audience is for fans of business sims, and why there is a greater focus on the business side compared to lighter examples out there. However, just because your game is meant for advanced players doesn't absolve you of looking at the UI/UX and how approachable it is and why the developers made changes after getting feedback.

What can make approachability elements hard to study for new designers is the fact that they are often invisible to the experience. Returning to the concept of "quality of life" features in a game, they are not the parts that the consumer is going to be thinking about. To study approachability, when you are playing any game, see if you can spot details that make it easy to keep playing the game, and pay attention if you must do something that puts the rest of the game on hold and whether there is a solution to make it quicker.

Another approachability feature that can be easy to spot is repetitive actions – where the player must continually stop what they're doing and repeat something repeatedly before they can get back to the task at hand. An often-seen example is when the player must pick up items and resources after a battle even if said resources don't take up inventory space, and there is never a reason to avoid them. Solutions include the use of dynamic commands, hotkeys, and the UX of a game. Anytime you are watching playtesters or playing the game yourself and you find that people are repeating the same thing that is separate from the core gameplay loop, see if you can shorten and remove this interaction.

Further up, I mentioned the "sort" feature in ARPGs to reduce the amount of time the player has to be away from the main screen. Another example that started with ARPGs but has also been borrowed by other games is having a designated "heal" option that can be accessed whenever the player wants. In older games, the norm was to always fill the inventory with healing potions, so that the player could rapidly heal if they were in any danger. This also meant having to set up a command or fumble through the inventory during combat to use a potion in the heat of the fight.

With *Diablo 2* (released in 2000 by Blizzard Entertainment), they went as far as to give the player belts that potions had to be added manually and use hotkeys to activate each slot, with the largest belts holding 16 potions (shown as a 4x4 grid) at one time. While this gave players a lot of means of healing, it still slowed the game down and required them to always have max potions ready before doing any kind of content. In *Diablo 3*, the player no longer had to buy or equip healing potions. Going forward, the player had one rechargeable potion always available and equipped. Instead of limiting the player based on the number of potions they could have, it was changed so that the player could heal at any time, but the potion would go on cooldown before it could be used again. The challenge of knowing when to heal was kept but was streamlined to make the interaction around it faster.

A more recent approachability feature that developers have been using helps with potentially triggering or stressful content. This ranges game by- game but can include censoring content or situations that may be related to a real-life phobia. A good example from the game *Grounded* (released in 2022 by Obsidian Entertainment) is about exploring a backyard as kids shrunken to the size of bugs, and having to survive with giant bugs, such as spiders. To help people who have arachnophobia, the developers have an option to turn all spiders into floating blob monsters that are far less terrifying (Figure 4.16). This is important to consider not only in cozy games but any title where there can be something that can trigger a

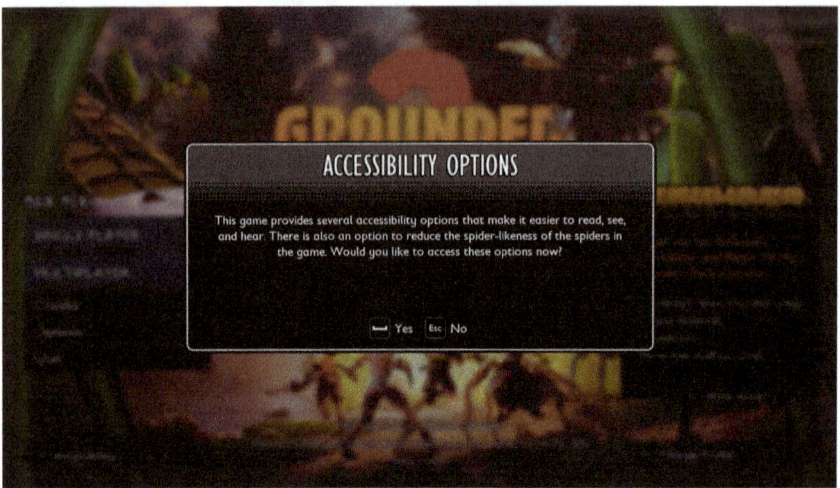

Figure 4.16

While *Grounded 2* (developed by Obsidian Entertainment and still in early access as of writing this book) is certainly not a cozy game, it's still one that the developers would like as many people to play. Part of improving both approachability and accessibility that started in the 2010s was paying more attention to gameplay elements that can cause stress or issues to people playing. Part of your core gameplay loop should not be knowingly triggering phobias in your player base… at least not without ample warning.

phobia. You can look up groups like the accessibility SIG mentioned earlier for more examples of content or game mechanics that can cause problems for people.

The advantage of indie games is that they are often heavily modified by fans to either add in new content or create mods to remove or alter issues that they didn't like. While some of these can be up for debate, there is an infinite number of mods out there specifically designed to improve the playability and approachability of a title. One of my all-time favorite games is the original *X-Com UFO Defense* (released in 1994 by Mythos Games and MicroProse). It is considered one of the best games of all time, but it is also one of the worst games to experience today going into it blind. Fans have been working on improvements and additional features for decades now. While the game is available for purchase via Steam, anyone who plays it today knows that the best possible version is using the program "OpenXcom" or the version known as "OpenXcom Extended that makes it far easier to play and install additional mods. There have been stories of games that were inspired by a popular game or mod because the designer didn't like something in the title and wanted to make a version of the game that fixes those complaints or goes in a different direction.

This entire chapter's focus on UI/UX design is meant to provide you with the tools to study a game and figure out what the developer's intent was with creating the experience. This can be applied to any game out there. If you choose to ignore these points, then you will be flying blind with your game, and while there are examples of games that seemingly ignored all conventional UI/UX and approachability practices and succeeded, they are often the exception to the rule.

When you are examining popular examples of a genre, just because the bestselling game has approachability issues does not excuse you from them with your game. Games that are the first successful take in a genre or subgenre have enough clout being the first that fans don't mind those issues; your game will not fare the same. Returning to *Stardew Valley*, I was not kidding about it being ground zero for the rise of farming-style games in the 2010s. Many of those games played like *Stardew*, but worse. You cannot just recreate someone else's game and expect it to be anywhere near the same level of success. Part of the reason why *Stardew* worked was that it built upon the formula of *Harvest Moon* and didn't stop with just copying that game to the letter.

One final topic about approachability once again comes back to hardcore fans vs. newcomers. This chapter has brought up the core gameplay loop of your game multiple times, and how approachability relates to it will be up to you to decide. As I've said, your most dedicated fans are going to enjoy your game warts and all, and they will often be the first to argue against approachability issues. A popular rebuke is "I don't find it annoying, so what's the problem?"

Figure 4.17

This is the last screenshot you would expect to find in a book about cozy games. This is from *Armored Core VI: Fires of Rubicon* (released in 2023 by FromSoftware) and the boss fight Balteus who appeared at the end of the first chapter of the game. This one fight became a rage point for many people, including those who have played FromSoftware's other difficult games. Forums turned into arguments over if this fight is too difficult or whether players need to get better at the game. The battle was eventually adjusted to the delight of the people who were stuck there and the dismay of those who beat it.

There is a difference between someone playing your game and fighting it due to approachability problems. This comes up repeatedly with discussions of game balance and difficulty and has been a constant tug of war with challenging games in the mainstream market, such as **soulslikes** (Figure 4.17). It should never be difficult to perform basic actions in a game period. If your core gameplay loop is about hardcore sword fighting, everything else that isn't focused on sword fighting should be intuitive and easy to perform. Even cozy and wholesome games are not immune to approachability problems, and frustration is felt even more in these games because their intent is supposed to be a relaxing experience.

Even in games that are considered hardcore, there are areas where approachability can be used to make things better. In *Elden Ring* (released in 2022 by FromSoftware), one of the early arguments for approachability was regarding having important characters and shops being automatically marked on the map once they've been located. Some of the hardcore fans argued that putting that in would "hurt the developers' vision of the game," but within a week or two of release, FromSoftware patched that feature in, as having to remember exactly where a character was located was not part of the core gameplay loop.

At the end of the day, you need to give the player a reason to play your game, and if you don't, they will not do it for you. Again, there's nothing wrong with saying your game is meant for a hardcore audience and balancing it as such, but there's a difference between understanding why someone plays a game and building it that way vs. making something purposely obtuse and frustrating that will drive all but your most hardcore fans away.

Note

1 https://www.wired.com/story/video-game-clickolding-oral-history/

5

Creating a Cozy (or Wholesome) Game

5.1 Defining Cozy, Wholesome, and Casual Design

Casual games and casual gaming are another bit of history that can be debated as to what game is "the first." On one hand, we could say that since the video game industry began in full of the likes of *Pong*, *Pac-man*, and the entire early arcade industry, they were casual games due to the simplicity of playing them.

On the other hand, what is defined as a casual game by fans today didn't really start to grow until the early 2000s and then exploded in popularity with the rise of mobile and browser gaming in the mid-2000s into the 2010s.

As I talked about the rise of the wholesome games movement, just because a game is meant for casual players doesn't make it wholesome or cozy. It's important to be able to set general guidelines that distinguish these subgenres from one another (Figure 5.1).

Casual design refers to games that are often easy to play and have low interactivity on the player's part. For a game like *Farmville*, someone is not playing the game for a mile a minute extreme challenge – they're placing down crops and buildings and waiting for things to finish. The appeal of popular casual and mobile games is the fact that they are very easy to start playing and get enjoyment out of

DOI: 10.1201/9781003646860-5

Figure 5.1

Understanding game design is about being able to see the unique qualifiers that make up different genres. People thought that all cozy games needed was to be for casual fans only, but the market has shown that you can do something different or more involved while still being cozy and wholesome about it.

them. As a quick tangent, studying the UI/UX of mobile games is a great way to see how fast these games can onboard players to their gameplay.

Both cozy and wholesome games are often casual in their gameplay, as they're meant to appeal to people looking for a relaxed experience, but they offer a different aesthetic to them. There are casual games all about fighting mutants, killing zombies, and watching things explode, and they would not be considered cozy or wholesome. Just having minimal gameplay is not enough in this respect, and there are countless indie games designed to be very easy to play but tell incredibly dark and mature stories. A newer trend in the middle of the 2020's has been the surge in popularity of "engine building" games – where the player is not directly interacting wit the game, but making choices that influence their score or outcome, with *Balatro* being the most popular example at this time. The appeal of engine builders has been creating a more casual take on roguelike design and focusing on decision making and choices as opposed to player action.

What can make things even harder is that coziness and wholesomeness are often defined by everyone differently. When I asked Matthew about what factors he thinks distinguish cozy from wholesome, he provided this answer:

> I like to think of wholesome games as hopeful. That's actually why we chose to use the term wholesome instead of cozy: a wholesome game can involve plenty of hardship or sadness, as long as there's a reason to be hopeful.

Regarding that point, I would like to propose the following qualifier regarding what makes a game cozy or wholesome. A cozy game is more about players having a relaxing time without the game providing a message or theme to take away. To recap *PowerWash Simulator*, players power wash anything and everything as per their client's request to earn money. It can be a relaxing game to zone out and enjoy the simple progression of taking a dirty residence and cleaning it from top to bottom. There is no serious plot to the game, no important lessons to learn, and that is fine. Numerous idle games also fall into cozy territory, with the recent trend of having idle games that only take up a quarter of the screen mentioned in Chapter 3.

A wholesome game, or more specifically what people consider wholesome, is meant to provide something more, oftentimes personal, for the player that they can take away from the experience. *Coffee Talk* was a game about running a coffee shop… that's it. There were no combat sections or struggles to pay your rent – you talked to customers, and you served coffee. What the game did was use this as a structure to tell personal stories about the lives of the people who become your regulars and the world that they live in. The games in the *To the Moon* series all have a theme of dealing with regret and coming to terms with death. There is emotion that comes with the best wholesome games that sticks with someone long after they finish the game.

When I asked Matthew about tips for making and writing a wholesome game, this was his response:

> Good art is personal, even if it's expressed through abstraction or metaphor. Tell the story you want to tell and let every design decision support that. That's my honest, boring answer. For those more interested in marketing or commercial art, the lesson from wholesome games (or any niche) is to consider your audience early and learn from them. What are they playing right now, and what do they enjoy about it? Be empathetic, because if you can't genuinely relate to your player, they'll see right through it.

This is often why wholesome games are meant to be personal, and why many designers will put some part of themselves into the game. This is not something that you can fake; again, given how specific this type of design is, people will know immediately if you are trying to mislead them.

A reason why the wholesome movement came from the indie space was that there are plenty of developers from diverse backgrounds who wanted to share a part of their lives and their culture with other people (Figure 5.2).

Whether your game is meant to be cozy or wholesome, there needs to be something that people can connect to, and that can vary from person to person. Just like how there is no perfect game, there isn't one game system or story that's going to resonate with every single player.

With this section, we are getting into the territory of splitting hairs trying to create a definable difference between cozy and wholesome games. Unlike the other genres and subgenres discussed in the *Deep Dive* series, there are no agreed-upon metrics for cozy and wholesome, with many people interchanging the terms at their leisure. This is not like discussing roguelike and roguelite design; both have

Figure 5.2

Dealing with loss is sadly something that affects everyone, and many creators will express that in different ways, such as *Pine: A Story of Loss* (released in 2024 by Made Up Games), that explores a widower learning to keep going and accept the loss of his wife.

specific design qualifiers that you must meet to call your game one. If you're planning on making something in either style, saying your game is cozy when it's wholesome or vice versa is not going to ruin it. The purpose of exploring this line of thought is to try and provide a little analysis to help you better frame and market your game. And not even Matthew, after helping curate wholesome and cozy games, has a set rule for the differences:

> For most players, I don't think there's a big difference between the two, and that's OK. From my perspective, wholesome is a bit broader artistically. A wholesome experience might include dark or troubling situations but with hope or the potential to make a positive impact. Cozy, on the other hand, is a more specific and deeply personal feeling. I've seen plenty of people describe games as cozy that don't feel that way to me, because the feeling comes from more than just the game—it's tied to personal associations and context.

Creating the mechanics and gameplay for a game to be cozy or wholesome is a different story, and it's what the rest of this chapter is going to focus on.

5.2 Setting Stakes

Throughout this book, we've talked about plenty of indie games and the aesthetics they are trying to pull off; getting that correct requires you to understand what kind of stakes and challenge you want for a cozy/wholesome game.

To recap, cozy/wholesome games focus on low-stakes design, meaning that there are no long-term consequences for messing up at any point (Figure 5.3). Some games, like *Stardew Valley*, will penalize the player short-term for running out of energy, but that is the extent of it, and the player is still free to continue playing as they did the next day. With long-term consequences, you should avoid any permanent consequences no matter how small they may be unless the player knows fully and well what they're getting into.

Creating a low-stakes experience is both about the story and gameplay of your title. From a story point of view, low-stakes games are never about the player, and by relation, the main character, being in any real danger or doing anything stressful. You can put the player in situations that in other games could be stressful or recontextualizing mechanics as I said with the undersea example in Section 4.2.

Platforming and jumping as a gameplay example can fit many different stakes based on the level design that they are paired with. For a challenging, high-stakes platformer, the player could be making jumps while dodging obstacles, lasers, spikes,

Figure 5.3

Thankfully for *Stardew Valley* fans, you'll never see something like this in the game. There's a difference between giving someone a challenge and having a high-stakes punishment in your game.

etc., and any mistake will send them back to the start. There are also plenty of games where platforming/being a platformer is simply the canvas for telling a story, and the platforming is kept very basic and easy to do with no penalty for missing a jump.

With gameplay, you want to avoid any kind of loss states, which again are conditions that a player would lose in a game. Let's take another stressful example of mountain climbing. There have been dozens of games dealing with mountain climbing, and of course, falling down said mountain. The most famous would be the rage game *Getting Over It with Bennett Foddy* (released in 2017). At any point, the player is at risk of launching themselves and going straight down and losing all their hard-earned progress. The constant fear of making a mistake would put it as far away from a cozy or relaxing game as one could get. Following the release, there is now a market and audience who specifically play these rage games at any chance they get.

However, there are ways of making this kind of game easier and lowering the stakes to target a different demographic. You could implement checkpoints that automatically put the player back where they were and adjust the control scheme to make it easier. Keep in mind that changing elements like this is also changing the aesthetics of your game, and in return, you are changing who the core audience of it will be. For the opposite of *Getting Over It*, there was the mountain climbing game *A Short Hike*, which has no long or short penalties for anything.

It is also possible to try and have it both ways by creating an experience that can be tuned for casual or hardcore play. The most popular way is providing accessibility features that turn off fail states or let the player skip difficult or demanding content. In *Celeste* (released in 2018 by Maddy Makes Games), it is known as one of the most challenging 2D platformers commercially released. However, the game can also be played with infinite lives, infinite jumps, and invincibility, to remove any challenge for people who just want to see the story.

However, as the designer, it is still your responsibility to set the tone and aesthetics for your primary audience – just putting in easier settings into a hard game or vice versa doesn't automatically double your consumer base (Figure 5.4).

Another aspect of designing for low stakes beyond limiting punishment and loss states is giving the player the freedom to change their mind with little consequences. There are plenty of games, both narratively and mechanically, that require the player to make long-lasting decisions or those that could immediately doom their play, such as with roguelike/roguelite design. Tough decision-making is part of the appeal of playing tactical and challenging games, but it's the opposite experience you want for a cozy game.

With that said, it doesn't mean that a good cozy game is "dumbed down"; you can have challenging and interesting choices within a low-stakes experience. In the game *Cauldron* (released in 2025 by Sleepydad Games), it combines low stakes with RPG and idle design. The player must fight groups of monsters to progress further in the world. These battles are reliant on the player being able to field the right combination of party members and abilities to counter the enemy. There are many examples of RPGs that limit the player's ability to rebuild their characters, also known as "respec," or require the player to pay a huge cost for the option to do

Figure 5.4

A misconception I've seen some developers and supporters of accessibility features make is thinking that assist modes and features can prevent churn spikes and problems from happening. While these features are great and do help, if someone is annoyed with your game or doesn't like it, they will stop playing even if you provide them with all the options in the world, and that is why you must still put in the effort when it comes to UI/UX. Even in Celeste, with the ability to literally disable any challenge in it, it still lost 30% of the audience before finishing the first chapter.

so. Here, the player is free at any time to reset all their characters and change them to meet the current demand. In this respect, the game is not about punishing the player for having the wrong team composition but challenging them to figure out what is needed from fight to fight.

There have been arguments both for and against having the option to respec in a game. Some feel that it robs the player of having to make tough decisions, while others like the flexibility to know that their choices aren't set in stone. However, for cozy/wholesome games where the player shouldn't be stressed out about making choices, it is a no-brainer to include. To that point, decisions like this are also a part of what the core gameplay loop of your game looks like.

A common rule of game design is that if you want to condition the player to do something or use an item, you need to make it as easy as possible to do it and never punish them in any way. If there is a loss state, then it should only affect the immediate short-term play; i.e., the player must restart a fight and not carry any long-term consequences. With items, the easier it is to acquire something, the greater the chance the player will use it. There are many stories of gamers hoarding items, even to the detriment of the game, because they're afraid they won't be able to get another one.

From a narrative perspective, your story will also help set the stakes. There is a big difference in tone between the world ending and the ice-cream cake going to melt if the player messes up. That doesn't mean you can't have a serious story or explore an emotional topic, such as the *To the Moon* series, but it's about how it's handled and presented, which I'll return to this answer from Matthew about what he considers in a game to classify it as wholesome:

> I like to think of wholesome games as hopeful. That's actually why we chose to use the term wholesome instead of cozy: a wholesome game can involve plenty of hardship or sadness, as long as there's a reason to be hopeful.

We've seen minor controversies facing cozy games in the past, where a game that's targeting fans of low-stakes games has a section or storyline that goes into a darker place and changes the stakes of what's happening. If you have a game that's all about throwing parties for friends, and out of nowhere, one of the plotlines involves someone being violently attacked at one of your parties, that's a tonal whiplash that can upset the audience that was here just to put on cute parties. Returning to accessibility and approachability, this is why games that do feature whiplash moments can feature a trigger warning or even allow the player to skip something that may upset them.

Another mechanic to avoid when designing around low stakes is countdown timers that force the player to either move fast or decide before time is up. This is different from having goals that must be achieved within a time frame if you inform the player properly about how long they have left.

Just remember, everyone has their own view of what cozy and wholesome means to them, and as we discussed in the last section, it's not possible to set a 100% definitive definition that everyone agrees on. You need to communicate with both your marketing and the messaging and tone within the game to educate the consumer as to what this game is. Given the fact that wholesome games can touch on darker or more serious topics, we've seen games lately provide a content warning at the start to inform the person playing if there is anything that could be stress-inducing.

As I've said, cozy and wholesome games are a subgenre, which means you need to be extra attentive as to who you are trying to appeal to with your game. There is always a high- and low-stakes example of any game mechanic and system, and like with UI/UX, the best way to experience this yourself is to play different games in the genre.

And remember, if your game is designed around different goals and playstyles, you can have content that is a bit tougher or higher stakes to do it. Reaching Ginger Island in *Stardew Valley*, players can eventually unlock one final job board that features some of the hardest challenges in the game with time limits to get them done. At this point in playing, the people who are still invested are going to be the hardcore fans looking for that added challenge, and it being optional means that someone won't be forced to do something they don't want to (Figure 5.5).

Finally, the simplest way to figure out what your audience wants is to ask them. There are plenty of designers who use social media and their own forums, discord channel, or steam discussion board, to pitch ideas to their fans. This does not work for every game, and as the game's designer, you must still decide the direction that your game will go. However, this can be a great way to get community interaction and learn more about the preferences from your fans.

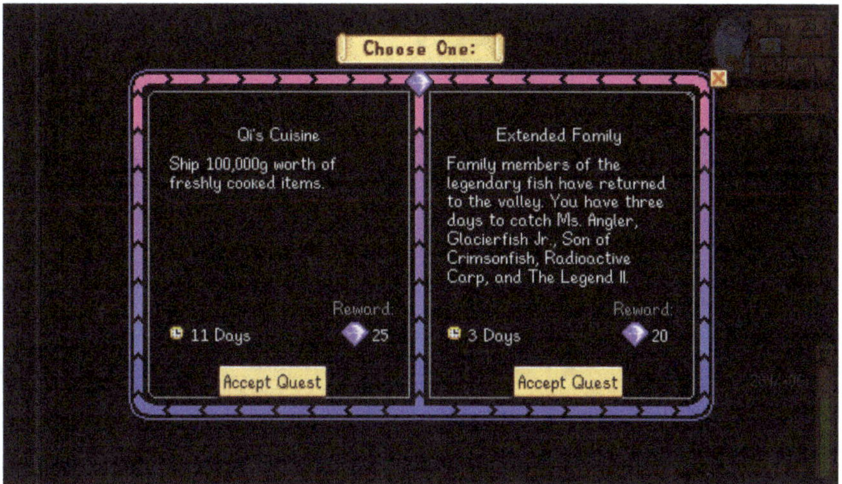

Figure 5.5

Ginger Island's job board provides the hardest challenges in the game, and that is why it's only accessible to players who are at the point where they are looking for something harder to do.

5.3 Exploring Sandbox Design

Throughout this book, I've touched on sandbox mode as another way to add low-stakes and cozy games to a genre, and it's time to talk a bit more about what that means from a design standpoint.

Sandbox mode is best used in games that offer an extensive amount of personalization and customization, and that is why the survival/crafter genre has had the most examples of it featured (Figure 5.6). Some games will have a dedicated sandbox mode that can be turned on, while other games can allow the player to create one through the game settings. For many survival games and those built on procedural generation, they may allow the player to adjust settings before the world is generated. This can include everything from resource density, the number of enemies, negative or positive events, and much more. With enough settings tweaked, it is possible for the player to create their own version of sandbox play, but it is considered good practice for the genre to have a setting already created. Another way to view sandbox mode is like playing a game with all cheat codes that reduce or remove difficulty one at once. If your game has any systems designed to make things more challenging – hunger, thirst, equipment durability, etc., they would be disabled for sandbox play.

Not every game works well or can be designed around sandbox play. The most straightforward negative example would be any linear or story-driven experience with a fixed amount of gameplay. There are several factors that you can look at to decide whether you want to pursue this kind of gameplay:

Figure 5.6

Sandbox mode and personalization go hand in hand, and while not everyone is going to be interested, the ones that are can create some amazing works. These four images are all taken from *Minecraft* builds that people posted online.

1. Does your game offer a variety of means of personalizing the experience?
2. Do your mechanics afford creative ways of using them?
3. If your game is on the harder side, does it have appeal toward casual audiences?

As I discussed with *Stardew Valley*, *Minecraft*, and *Animal Crossing*, these games allow the player to personalize their experiences through their character, homes, and apparel. Any time that the player is allowed to build something piece-by-piece, this opens the door to personalization. Someone could just make a standard log cabin to stay in, or they could build their dream medieval castle one block at a time.

Personalization in this respect goes with creating a variety of assets for the player to use, such as different shirts, hats, wallpaper, tile color, lighting, and the list stretches infinitely on. In previous *Deep Dives*, when I detailed the variety of mods that can be created for games, no matter how many personalization options you have, there will always be people who want more. If you're building a game around personalizing the experience, then you should provide the player with a variety of ways of doing so, and most PC games that have these options will support modding functionality. With *Stardew Valley*, there are a multitude of mods, just focusing on the personalization side, which can change the look of everything – including the models and portraits of every character in the game.

Some developers will either ship at launch or release afterwards a software development kit (SDK) that provides players with a toolset to create and integrate content into their games. Other times, if the fans are invested enough, they may come together to create their own toolset. Depending on the game in question, some are designed to accept mods very easily, while others may require a launcher or mod loader that allows the game to load with them. There is far more to modding, with each game having its own challenges to make them work. If you're interested in learning more, the best thing would be to search for mods for your preferred game, and that should also lead you to the modding tools used.

However, there are two things to note when it comes to modding. The first is how mods will work in a multiplayer setting. Some games will require other players to download the mods to interact with the player with the installed mods. Other games will have it that everyone can play with each other, but only those with the respective mods installed will be able to see them. For games released on Steam, there is the option to set up Steam Workshop functionality, with the workshop acting as a one-stop for any and every submitted mod. Mods can be rated and curated by fans and provide an easy way for people to quickly and effortlessly install or remove mods from their games.

For multiplayer games, it is important to pay attention to the subject matter and content of said mods. There will unfortunately be people who will create mods that feature very sensitive content, and especially in a casual game, you don't want those mods or content to be seen by people who don't want that in their game.

On the matter of having mechanics that can be used in creative ways, this veers into immersive sim territory, which is a very specific form of game design (Figure 5.7). Immersive sims are about simulating the world and allowing the player to use mechanics and tools in ways not originally intended or set up by the designer. Immersive sims are built on interaction – how one mechanic or object interacts with everything else and can get advanced fast.

Let's imagine an example where the player can place copper wiring which if hit by electricity will conduct it. On the surface, that doesn't sound all that exciting, but if it interacts with the world and other objects, there are many applications for this:

- The player could wire their own personalized house to have electric lighting
- Wiring could be run to water to create electrical traps for enemies
- With machines that could push or pull when activated, it could be possible to create even more advanced machines or machinations

An important rule for developers is to never underestimate what players can do if you provide the right tools. You do need to be mindful of what is something the player could do if they want vs. what is required by the game. Taking *Minecraft* as an example, the level of interaction between different elements and tools grew steadily over the years. There are people who created intricate devices and setups and those who completely ignored them. With the electricity example mentioned, *Minecraft* has its own version of this in the form of "redstone circuits" that can be set up to run electrical currents throughout your world, which in the grand scheme

Figure 5.7

Immersive sim design can be hard to describe, and just showing a screenshot won't do much justice either. This is a screenshot from *Besieged* (released in 2020 by Spiderling Studio). The catapult pictured here is not created and shipped with the game. This is something designed by the editing tools with each part on it meant to emulate a real catapult and simulate the physics that go with launching an object with it. With a game like *Besieged*, the player is required to interact with the objects and tools at this level of detail, while other games may have it as an option for advanced play.

of playing is entirely optional to use. If you are going to require the player to make use of advanced techniques with your different objects, then you must provide onboarding to teach them about it.

Providing multiple gameplay options can also act as a way of giving players of different skill levels a means of enjoying the game. With factory/automation games, there are people who will use every advanced mechanic and tool to create a Rube Goldberg-styled machine that works flawlessly, and there will be people who just use the basic elements and that's it. In this respect, neither way of playing is considered "correct"; they'll both accomplish the player's task, but no one is being punished if they didn't build their factory "this way." In games about having specific playstyles or builds, having easier to learn builds will allow lesser-skilled players the ability to enjoy the game and assist the other players who may be using harder characters to play.

For the third point, this one comes up when talking about survival crafters or any game that has a mix of fans who prefer personalizing the world and those who are in it for a challenge. While hardcore purists may not like the idea of having a sandbox mode, this does open your game to a wider audience who are there to hang out with friends, build a variety of structures, and don't want to have to worry about starving or being killed by bad guys (Figure 5.8).

Figure 5.8

Multiplayer is another system that goes well with sandbox modes. For something like the *Minecraft* examples posted at the start of this section, some of the larger projects could only be completed in a reasonable time with the help of other players. For survival crafters, multiplayer also means that if someone is good at building, they can handle that task while other players can do something else. The game on the right is *Don't Starve Together* (released in 2016 by Klei Entertainment). A multiplayer-focused follow-up to the base game; being able to play it with friends not only became an appealing option, but it is higher rated than the base game.

A distinction that needs to be made is how sandbox mode thrives in open-ended games. A linear game is one where there is a fixed endpoint and average length and is a part of the pacing in most games. Open-ended games don't have a fixed length; they may have an intended end or goal to achieve, but how and when a player gets there is entirely up to them. With everyone experiencing the game differently, it means that there is no one "right way to play." For games built on fixed lengths and challenges, making them easier or harder comes down to understanding the mechanics and how to influence them. With sandbox mode, you are technically turning off parts of your game mechanics, and the reason why this is okay in this example is that your game should appeal to different audiences. *Minecraft* would have never achieved the same level of success if it didn't have its creative mode.

There will be people who will only play your game at the highest level of difficulty; they may even install mods to make it harder than what you originally intended, and that's fine. Just as you can have an audience who just wants to build things, see the story, and doesn't want to worry about dying and losing progress, and once again, that's an acceptable way to play. The more options players have to play your game, the easier it will be to be experienced by a larger market and help its chances to succeed.

One final point I want to clarify is that open-ended gameplay in and of itself is different from sandbox. With *Stardew Valley*, I've brought up multiple times how a huge part of its appeal is the fact that players have multiple ways of progressing and moving through the game. However, the player is still required to earn money and increase their level in each profession if they want to see everything. There are mods available that do remove those requirements, and that would be an example of sandbox gameplay.

Personalization and creativity go together, and when it works, it can greatly extend the interest and reach of any game. The *Animal Crossing* example mentioned in Chapter 3 was one of the biggest cases when a game blew up outside of its normal audience and helped people during the stressful time of the heights of COVID-19. There are schools that use sandbox and creative modes in games like *Roblox* and *Minecraft* for lessons or as an outlet for their students to make something with. From a marketing perspective, if your game can create a variety of personalized elements, that is something you should put front and center in any trailers or marketing you send out.

At the end of the day, sandbox modes are about letting someone be free to create whatever they want and can put as much or as little into it as they choose. While most people may never consider doing something as intricate as recreating the Earth in *Minecraft*, once again, never doubt the determination of fans of a game to get very creative with their projects (Figure 5.9).

Figure 5.9

In case you thought I was making this up, these screenshots are from the fan project "Build the Earth," with the goal of recreating the Earth in *Minecraft*, and has been going on for several years now. For more about the project, or if you want to join them, visit: https://buildtheearth.net

5.4 A Relaxing Progression Curve

Progression comes part and parcel with your core gameplay loop – how does someone move through your game? How do things grow and/or escalate over the course of playing?

When we examine reflex-driven or high-stakes games, progression is defined by escalation – new enemies, new bosses, obstacles; the challenge is supposed to grow. There is also the concept of the power curve – becoming more powerful through leveling up or unlocking new abilities. With this book focusing on low-stakes games, in return, the progression curve is a bit different to go with the expectations of the fans (Figure 5.10).

> Many wholesome games center on player progression and collection, which can be seen as a kind of escalation, even if the physical challenge doesn't increase. Beyond that, I think players are often motivated by the desire to create or immerse themselves in a world or see a story through to the end.
>
> **– Matthew Taylor**

The most common example of progression is the story of your game. For narrative-focused games, you are building your gameplay based on the narrative you are telling. In effect, the length of your game is measured by the length of your plot.

Figure 5.10

Progression means different things depending on the game and genre. With *Gone Home* (released in 2014 by Fullbright), the story is what moves the player through to explore the home, with puzzles being the obstacle in the way of solving the mystery. Scale-based progression is not the same as adding more depth. The player is still doing the same thing, just a lot more of it, as we see with the avalanche of shards from *(the) Gnorp Apologue* (released in 2023 by Myco).

When interviewing developers who have focused on narrative games, a common point is that more is not better in this respect – if your story can be told in 30 minutes, then you have a 30-minute game. Story-focused games will often not focus on gameplay, or they will have gameplay sections that are fixed in terms of what the player is doing. Puzzles are often featured to provide something to test the player that is not reflex-driven. However, making a story-driven game means that said story must be the focus – if players are getting frustrated or stuck at something that is preventing them from experiencing the plot, then that must be carefully examined and adjusted. This is why games built on low stakes that have puzzles or some element of challenge will often offer the player the option to skip or auto-solve a puzzle or section if they are completely stuck.

Artifex Mundi, which I mentioned in Chapter 3, did just that with every one of their hidden object games. For every hidden object or puzzle in the game, there was a timer ticking down while someone was attempting to solve it. When time's up, the player was given the option for the game to automatically solve the puzzle or challenge and move on with the story.

While this may sound counterintuitive for people who traditionally play high-stakes games, remember, the point of a low-stakes game is to relax and not stress out. If someone is stuck or frustrated at any point in your game, then it is failing at being cozy/wholesome.

For titles where there are gameplay and goals to achieve, even with the lower stakes, there is still a progression curve that drives the game forward. For linear games, they will often follow a chapter format – each chapter of the game will require the player to complete X number of tasks that can be done whenever the player chooses. When all the tasks are complete, the game will advance to the next chapter, the story moves forward, and new tasks are introduced. Given the low-stakes nature of cozy/wholesome games, it's rare to see a loss state; instead, the player is given as many chances as they need to progress.

This is also similar to the progression seen in automation games. The player's goal is to reach ever higher unlocks on the technology tree or tech tree. Each new tier can be treated as its own "chapter," but instead of unlocking a new story, it focuses on unlocking new technologies and resources the player must use to continue progressing.

Due to the relaxing nature of cozy/wholesome games, many of them adopt a progression curve that is popular among idle games in the form of scaling. Rather than making things harder or more demanding from the player's input, idle games use the attraction of growth to provide progression and motivation to keep playing (Figure 5.11).

Here's an example: When a player starts an idle game, all they can do is click on something to make resources. This is slow, boring, and for people with repetitive stress injuries, can be painful to do. The very first purchase in any idle game will be automating this action; while yes, this is slower than clicking, the player is no longer forced to do so to progress. From there, each new upgrade or purchasable item will scale up in terms of the resources required to buy them and the

Figure 5.11

Scale has been a popular form of progression used in many games, thanks to how easy it is to show growth. You can use it in a game like *Cookie Clicker*, or with increasing productivity with my jam-making shack in *Stardew Valley*.

amount of resources they will produce. Going from 0 to 1,000 is going to be slow the first time, but eventually, the player will be earning millions of resources every second.

Cozy games may not get that far in terms of resources earned, but they will use the tier system mentioned in Section 3.4 as a way of giving the player a sense of progress and scale. If the player is running a restaurant, the tiers could be something like this:

- Tier 0 – Cup of water
- Tier 1 – French fries
- Tier 2 – Burger
- Tier 3 – Cheeseburger
- Tier 70 – Golden lobster served with platinum butter on diamond plates

Part of using scaling as a form of progression is how the game handles the existence of the lower tiers. Some titles will still require lower-tier goods and resources as part of the production chain to make something better: To create a gold sword, the player must produce a silver sword and combine that with a gold bar, but to produce a silver sword, the player must first make a bronze sword and combine that with a silver bar.

This always keeps resources relevant but doesn't provide a reward for moving up in tiers of production. Other games will say that each new tier requires different resources than the previous – once the player is making tier 3 goods, they no longer need to keep producing lower tiers, or the lower-tier resources and production chains will not interact with any subsequent tiers.

An example I liked that I would like to see more developers copy was from the game *Nova Lands* (released in 2022 by Behemutt). For reaching certain research goals, the game would remove the requirement of lower tier materials from producing goods or structures, allowing the player to free up that space for other things.

Mechanic-based progression only works when the new content is not just a reskin of another task. If chopping down 20 trees is functionally the same as chiseling 20 statues, the player's reward for doing work is simply more work. As with the *Nova Lands* example, you can use advanced mechanics and rewards as a way to mitigate or remove the earlier ones, provided that you can still give the player something to do. The late-game challenges of the game switch from building and producing resources on the planet to furnishing and supporting a space station with its own resource requirements, challenges, and rewards to unlock.

Returning to *Stardew Valley* and other good examples of using scale, each new tier and type of good brought with them their own set of mechanics and processes to create them. Refining ore is different from raising animals, which is different from producing wine. If you can make each tier its own subsystem rather than copying what's already there, it will be more engaging to do.

The other advantage of this method is that it keeps up with the low stakes of cozy/wholesome games. What the player is doing is not getting progressively harder but just introducing new things that act as different rewards to go after. And again, there should not be any long-term penalties or fail states for not doing something quick enough.

As *Stardew Valley* is an example of an open-ended game, it's important to touch on what makes open-ended design different from other games with its progression. The tier system of unlocking new items and things to produce is a part of it, but again, open-ended games are about allowing the player multiple ways of achieving a goal. These ways can differ in terms of optimization and difficulty, which can create different strategies for specific playstyles such as the hardcore side of playing a cozy game like *Stardew Valley* that I mentioned earlier. There are people who have done challenges in the game, such as: No farming, not using the mines, only earning money through livestock, and more.

The reason why these challenges can work is that while *Stardew Valley* has strict goals for progression, the means of reaching them are not. Here is a hypothetical example of how a game can do two goals:

- Earn 50,000 gold
- Create 3,000 rugs

The first goal can be achieved by doing literally anything within the game that earns the player money; once again, if the player does it fast or slow is beside the point. With the second goal, there is no wiggle room to do something else – if the game demands 3,000 rugs, the player must create 3,000 rugs. In *Stardew*, the different skill paths require the player to perform tasks related to them, but it never restricts the player's ability to earn experience based on their progress in the skill.

You can still have progress gates that both act as a goal for the player to shoot for and something that moves the game forward once it's accomplished. *Stardew Valley*'s example is getting access to Ginger Island, and as I covered, it is a completely different biome with its own resources, challenges, and the way to the true ending of the game. Unlocking it requires the player to either completely go through the Joja Mart storyline or finish the community center challenges before the player can get access to it. Within those two storylines, there are multiple ways of getting the goods or enough money to complete them, and all those paths will lead to the player reaching Ginger Island.

The use of scale can also provide a bit more challenge if players want to pursue them (Figure 5.12). As I mentioned earlier, *Stardew Valley's* ultimate ending requires the player to achieve max completion, which is completing every single possible task within the game. One of which is to acquire the gold clock – which is priced at 10 million gold and is the most expensive purchase. The only way to earn enough money in a reasonable time is to massively scale up production to earn more money. Players have another option if they just want to focus on earning money and not the specific tasks. They can spend 500,000 gold to earn 1% of completion per purchase. While this may sound like a lot of money for so little

Figure 5.12

Stardew Valley does have rewards players can go for at the end game. Besides the gold clock on the left, there are the obelisks that require a lot of money and rare resources. By constructing them, the player can warp to those specific areas, cutting down on travel time. At the point they would be unlocked, the player should have access to nearly everything, but this acts as a small quality of life improvement to go with the prestige of constructing one.

progress, the players who get to this point are easily earning that amount of money regularly to make use of it.

And again, it's important to note that for games that appeal to different play styles, everyone will have their own definition of reaching "the end." There are people who will never touch Ginger Island, care about 100%, and are only there to see the story conclusion with the various villagers. For open-ended games, you need to be careful with how you combine play styles and mechanics. For instance: requiring someone to do a heavy combat section if they want to see how a storyline finishes when combat was not a part of it prior. If you force someone to do gameplay they don't like to finish the parts they do, they are going to end up hating the experience.

Another example of having open-ended, but fixed goals would be automation games. In the game *Dyson Sphere Program* (currently in early access by Youthcat Studio), the player's ultimate goal is to build a Dyson sphere, which will require a variety of resources and items created. The gameplay loop works like this:

- Players harvest resources
- Players refine resources into usable items and science cubes
- Science cubes are spent unlocking new technologies

Each set of technologies can be unlocked in whichever order the player chooses, but moving to the next set requires them to set up the industry and automation required to construct the necessary science cubes. The game begins at the local level setting up factories, then global, with the player setting up factories and harvesting resources on the starting planet. The first big jump involves going into space and setting up factories within the solar system itself. Eventually, the player will start making intergalactic travel and set up factories across the known universe. In this way, the player's progress through the game is fixed to these milestones, but how they achieve them is entirely up to them. New technologies allow the player to create higher-tiered goods and make it easier to create the older tiers.

Open-ended goals can work, such as with automation games, provided the player understands the basics. You still need to onboard the player on how your mechanics work before you cut them loose. The best way to create an open-ended goal is to tell the player they need "X," and X can be acquired or achieved through multiple methods (Figure 5.13). The more ways available, the more freedom the player has to explore the game space. *Forager* has two goals – earning money and leveling up, with both intertwined. Anything the player does earns experience, allowing them access to new buildings and methods for exploring. Items created or found can be sold for money, and the player can also construct structures that create money on a timer. As the amount of money and experience progressively increases, the player must move on to further ways to increase the amount of each they're earning. In turn, whatever progress the player is making in one goal affects the other, and they are never doing anything that would be considered unproductive.

Figure 5.13

Automation design is all about figuring out how to make something more optimized for the task at hand. In this screenshot from *Dyson Sphere Program*, I decided to consolidate all my basic item production into one factory segment that would then ship out the completed goods all over to where they're needed – turning my starting planet into one giant automation machine. This is certainly not the required way to do it, and everyone has their own way of achieving their goals.

The other advantage of having a goals-based progression is that it allows you as the developer to know exactly where the player is in terms of ability and knowledge of the game at any given point. This allows you to create challenges or goals at different skill levels and to push the player forward, if need be, to different objectives.

A frequent example of early-game goals is teaching the player to perform common tasks – gather five vegetables, build a chest for the first time, cook a meal. These goals are designed to teach the player the basics of a game and are the foundational lessons to do more. Often, goals of this nature are used in place of a formal tutorial – you're not telling the player to do X, Y, or Z, but offering them a reward for learning and doing them. The major goals that either move the story along or unlock a new part of the tech tree require the player to understand all the mechanics leading up to it and will reward the player with the next step of the game.

One of the best idle games was *Cookie Clicker* by Orteil (first released in 2013) which received additional content and improvements over the years to create new ways of progressing. In the latest version, each one of the game's tiers introduces a subsystem that the player can explore – farms allow them to grow crops that provide bonuses; the banks unlock an actual stock market to use.

Knowing that there is something new coming or that a task will reward the player with X motivates them to keep playing. You can have games where the motivation is strictly story-based, and that has its own specific fanbase, but the best games manage to provide both gameplay and story progression. The player should always feel like they are moving forward in the game; whether it's by miles or millimeters. While some games can get away with long-term punishments and setting the player backwards, that is not the case for cozy and wholesome titles. A cozy game where someone can end up in a worst position than they were at when they started is not a game for a relaxing and low-stakes time.

With the progression of your game, it must match the length of the game systems. There is a trap that designers fall into when the player has nothing new to unlock or go after, but the game is still going. With *PowerWash Simulator*, by the time the player has accumulated enough stars and money to unlock the final power washer/equipment upgrade, there are still more missions to do; the only remaining upgrade is saved for the final story mission, but there will be multiple missions in the game's final set where there will be no more equipment to buy. Once all the upgrades are purchased, there are no additional progression goals to achieve or act as mid-/long-term rewards. This is not the same as the player finishing the game and then trying to go for 100% completion, but the main path is still going, and there are no more goals other than to finish the game. If your game is built on progression around introducing something new, you shouldn't go through multiple missions or hours of gameplay without anything new.

Returning to *Plants vs. Zombies*, there was always a reward for finishing a story level. No matter how small or impactful that reward may be, the player always knows they're getting something for making progress. And this also acts as another method of onboarding – waiting on introducing more advanced elements via the reward system for players who get far enough into the game to prove that they are ready for it.

The other problem with progression is if the game is too slow to get the player invested. With automation and idle games, I've already talked about how these games start out slowly before improvements are introduced. You do not want the player to be stuck playing the game the worst way for long, and why the first upgrade is often one that removes a problem. With idle games, it's being able to earn resources without clicking. There is a difference between giving the player something new and exciting vs. fixing or mitigating an issue that is annoying. The reason why *Stardew Valley* is praised for its gameplay is that it presents rewards and upgrades fast (Figure 5.14).

The sprinkler example I mentioned in Section 3.4 acts as both a new tool and a fix for the annoyance of watering crops by hand. As the player scales up their operation, the starting sprinkler will not be able to keep up, and that is why there are two additional tiers that cover more space that unlock at higher levels of farming. This goes with another important part of progression – being able to see where the player began and where they are now. At the start of *Stardew Valley*, maintaining 20 crops can be time-consuming; at the end of the game, players can be managing hundreds of crops easily with all their upgrades.

Figure 5.14

Stardew Valley's rewards and upgrades add more things to do but will also add ways of reducing the time spent on them. With farming, it can be slow to plow the land and water all the different plots. However, by the end of the game, a fully upgraded hoe and iridium sprinklers allow you to do mass farming with ease.

Good progression systems are there from the very beginning, and the player must always feel like they are making progress in some capacity. When the player is required to do repetitive tasks with the only reward being at the very end, that's when we refer to something as a "grind" in relation to gameplay. Grinding can be reduced if the player is able to perform multiple tasks to achieve the same goal, or that by performing the task, they are making progress in other areas. *Stardew Valley's* mastery challenge could be considered a grind by the fact that the experience required dwarfs everything previously. However, since the game is factoring any and all experience earned, it means that the player doesn't have to stop what they're normally doing to work on mastery, and instead, they are still being rewarded for playing the game.

Since idle and cozy design are often paired together, idle games have a different way of motivating the player to keep going with a restart mechanic. This has different names to it, some use prestige, ascension, resetting, and other terminology. What they all have in common is that the player restarts their entire save file, losing all resources, upgrades, and returning to square one. By doing so, they will unlock additional content and a special resource that persists across upgrades that increase the resource generation. This allows players to get further with each reset and see more of the game. Advanced examples may tie new gameplay systems and challenges to reaching different amounts of the resource. However, this form of progression only applies to idle design and would not fit in a game built around a final goal or story progression.

An exception to that last point is with "short form" idle or incremental games. Another take that has been growing in popularity are idle and incremental games built on a story or a fixed end. Instead of requiring dozens or hundreds of hours, both on and off the game, someone can see the ending within about 3-5 hours of play. In this way, the player is getting the experience of playing one of these games, but with the knowledge that it's not something they are going to have to play daily for weeks or months to get to the end.

Figuring out your progression is also about determining what the end of your game looks like. With some games, the end is quite literally the final cutscene, the final stage, etc. For open-ended titles like *Stardew Valley*, while there is the true ending of reaching 100%, the nonlinear nature means that you can set your own goals to achieve if you choose to ignore it (Figure 5.15). For instance, speedrun challenges and limitations to earning money mentioned earlier in this book are examples of this.

Something I bring up in other *Deep Dives* is the notion of the "final test" – the last section of the game designed to test the player's mastery over the mechanics. For cozy/wholesome games that don't feature escalation along these lines, the ending may just be one final level that is like the ones that came before it, or the final bit of story to wrap up the plot. The original perfection challenge in *Stardew Valley* was considered to be the final test of the main story, and the updates that eventually brought 100% as the true ending would be considered "post-game" challenges.

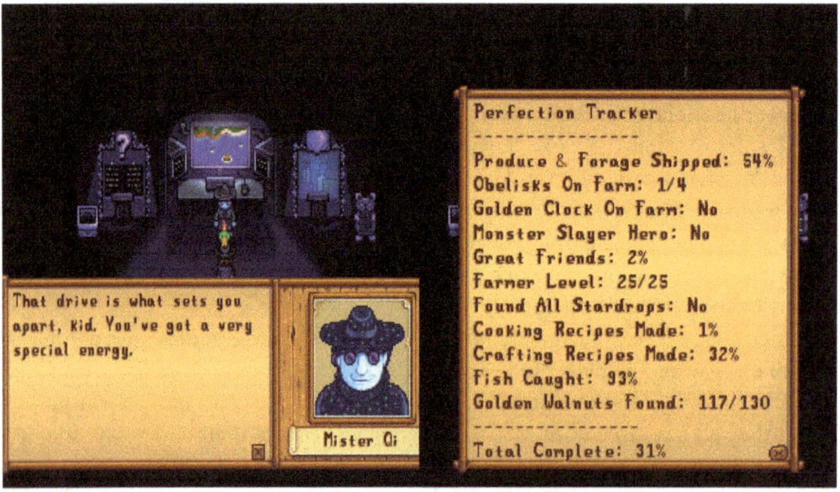

Figure 5.15

There is a difference between required and optional challenges from the player's perspective. The "normal" path through your game is going to be treated as what must be done, while optional content is something for the truly dedicated. With *Stardew Valley's* perfection goal, only the players who are going for everything will ever see it, and by that point, there's a good chance they'll keep playing for it.

Another point about creating a progression curve is player-defined challenges – when someone has a specific goal to achieve that is their "end game." All the challenge runs of *Stardew Valley* fit in this section; however, you can have player-defined goals that are far simpler. For a game about building, maybe someone just wants to build a mansion or a castle and that's all they want out of the game. While having your game be open enough to accommodate these goals is great, it doesn't absolve you from still defining the beginning, middle, and end of your game. You can market a game as just a sandbox/blank slate for the player to interact with if you so choose. Some developers may tease the player to go after specific goals in the form of achievements, but those aren't required.

Progression is different for every game, and you cannot just directly copy another game's progression system and expect it to work just the same. As you're designing, think about what the intended end of your game is and how does someone get there. Even in the most open-ended games, there will come a point when the player has seen everything, done everything, and there is no new content that the game can provide. Some people will reach that and still want more; others would have stopped a long time before. You want as many people as possible who have played your game to be leaving it satisfied with the experience, because that's what's going to get them to come back for your next game.

Length is no longer considered a metric for quality of a game, not just with story-focused ones. Just adding content to pad out playtime never works. With cozy/wholesome games, they can be short enough to tell a story or provide hours of entertainment for someone who wants to be in that world.

> My favorite wholesome game of all time is *A Short Hike*, and that's a pretty short game, especially if you don't collect all the extras. On the other hand, folks spend hundreds of hours in games like *Stardew Valley* or *Animal Crossing*. Ultimately, games are art, and although some players may judge a game's value based on its length, I don't think it's a factor in its quality, regardless of genre.
>
> **– Matthew Taylor**

With regard to post-release support, such as the updates in *Stardew Valley*, this is entirely up to the designer and comes with pros and cons. Adding more content to a game can extend its shelf life and bring in new fans. However, the added cost of creating such content can eat into any profits earned from that game. In *Stardew's* case, with the game earning so much revenue, working on new content is not going to hurt the success of it (Figure 5.16). For smaller games or those that just barely broke even, it is a far riskier prospect. It is rare for a game that just sold poorly or averagely to see a huge bump thanks to additional content. And as I've talked about, for story-focused games, new content wouldn't fit the game's pacing.

It's important if you decide to take this route to understand what kind of content you want to make and how long you are going to continue to support the game. When creating DLC or new updates for a game, there are two broad categories of content. Supplemental content is meant to fit within the game to flesh out preexisting systems and mechanics and doesn't directly add more length to the

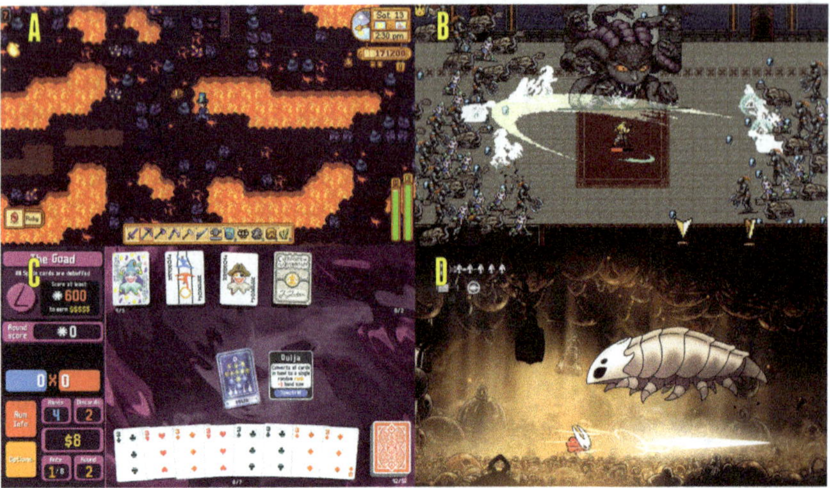

Figure 5.16

Behold, the four horsemen of games so successful they can keep getting post-release support. This is something reserved for developers who have a massive success and, unfortunately, not feasible for a lot of indie studios. (A: *Stardew Valley*, B: *Vampire Survivors*, C: *Balatro*, D: *Hollow Knight Silksong*)

game. This can include new cosmetics, new ways of earning money or resources, new dialogue options, and so on. Games that are meant to be replayed, such as roguelikes, benefit more from supplemental content to add more variety to their runs. Brand new content that adds more to the game will extend the amount of time someone can play, and includes new levels, areas, quests, etc. *Stardew Valley*, as we've talked about, is an example of a game that features both kinds of content with its major updates.

Unless you are creating new story content, such as in live service games, there will be a point regardless of the money you are making that you will run out of things to add. There's nothing wrong with ending support for a game, and it's rare for one game to sustain a studio indefinitely. And finally, don't feel like because another game has months or years of post-release support that you should be pressured to do the same. If there's room and interest to add more and you feel like doing it, then go for it. However, there is nothing wrong with releasing a game, putting out any big fixes and technical support, and moving on to your next project.

5.5 Is Everything Cozy (or Wholesome)?

While trying to define cozy and wholesome games, I've discussed throughout this book how these genres are more thematic than mechanical, and I want to talk about what that means from a game design perspective.

Game mechanics are not predefined to any aesthetic. Let's take FPS; when I use the phrase "FPS," your mind may immediately think of high-stakes, ultra-violent, shooters with giant guns filling screens with bullets and explosions. However, the very same mechanics could also be used for games about photographing wildlife, throwing paint on a wall to create murals, or the aforementioned power washing everything.

With the game *Ooblets* (fully released in 2022 by Glumberland), there was combat in the form of deck-building and using cards against your opponent. Where many other deck builders focused on cards and the aesthetics of combat and killing, all the cards in *Ooblets* were centered around a dance-off, with the side earning the most points from the audience "winning" the fight. Another example with card-based combat would be *My Card is Better Than Your Card!* by Utu Studios (still in development at the time of drafting this book), which focuses on schoolyard card battles with adorable stickers and characters.

To go back to the core gameplay loop, you need to decide what actions someone is going to do in your game and how they relate to the aesthetics and UX you're aiming for. The purpose of your mechanics and their implementation will directly affect the aesthetics of your game, and whether it can be labeled as cozy or wholesome.

> Thinking of games as art, it makes more sense to me to categorize them by how they make you feel, rather than how you literally play them. Pokémon Snap and Halo are both first-person shooters, but they elicit such different emotions, and to me, emotion is the most important aspect when we talk about art.
>
> **– Matthew Taylor**

One of the early popular casual game concepts was running a restaurant or some kind of food service industry. The player had to take dishes to the correct customers to win. Over the years, we've seen games that have explored the importance of food and culture to make them wholesome, expanded the cooking and restaurant experience to make them cozy, or focus on the depth and craziness of running a restaurant to make a hardcore challenging example (Figure 5.17).

The depiction of monsters or characters in your game can also affect the perception of it. Zombies and vampires can be scary creatures, or they can be cute and adorable, suffering emotional problems and trauma, and everything in between.

In every *Deep Dive*, I've said that you should not treat mechanics and their use as fixed elements that only work one exact way. Doing something different with a game system is how we've seen surprising successes over the 2010s to now.

What you must do is draw a line in the sand as to what your experience is going to be. You cannot say that your game is a relaxing, nail-biting, cozy, extremely difficult, scary, romantic, and a wholesome experience about gruesome murder. Given how specific the fan base is for cozy and wholesome, trying to throw every idea you have into one is how you end up with an unrefined mess.

This book has been noticeably lighter compared to the previous entries on design theory, and you may think that designing a cozy or wholesome game is

Figure 5.17

Mechanics by themselves do not create the aesthetic or tone of your game, but how they are implemented. With these three games, each one is about serving food, but they couldn't be further apart. *Diner Dash* (left), was popular during the heights of the casual mobile market craze, with very little connection to the act of cooking. *Cook, Serve, Delicious* (middle) was a hardcore example forcing players to respond quickly to orders and made it challenging to cook. While *Venba* (right) is a wholesome puzzle game of trying to figure out how to cook food from incomplete recipes.

about purposely making a limited gameplay experience, but you can have more involved gameplay mechanics depending on the genre. Because we are talking about thematic genres, the aesthetics of the action are just as important as the gameplay itself. Earlier in this section, I mentioned *Ooblets* as a game that features the mechanics related to combat but changed the aesthetics around it. With a game like *Stardew Valley*, the player is given the choice to actively go out and fight and defeat monsters, and there is an entire system and progression related to combat.

I brought up *Stardew Valley* when I was talking with Matthew about the use of combat in wholesome games and what his thoughts are related to having a form of fighting:

> I think it matters who you're fighting, why, and whether it's optional. There's a bit in our official FAQ that speaks to this: "If a game is violent, but that violence is about overthrowing an oppressor, is it unwholesome? We say no!" Games where combat

> feels shoehorned in just because it's a familiar mechanic are a little more boring to me, but many players enjoy oscillating between action-focused gameplay and something more chill and low-stakes. Stardew is a good example.

And *Stardew Valley* is the perfect example when discussing whether a cozy/wholesome game can be deep to play. Part of what led to the stigma behind calling games casual was that many browser-based and mobile games in the late 2000s/early 2010s, were targeting consumers with monetization in their casual games. They were designed to be very simple to play and get started, but then they introduce difficulty spikes and pain points to motivate someone to spend money. With the mobile market now courting core and hardcore gamers, we've seen an uptick in indie games that are being designed around a casual experience and being cozy or wholesome.

Just remember, people find different experiences cozy, wholesome, relaxing, stressful, and any other emotions you can think of. A game I enjoyed in 2025 was *Little Rocket Lab* by Teenage Astronauts. While the gameplay was built around automation and factory design, the developers combined that with a slice-of-life approach like *Stardew Valley*. Even though it's not the most advanced example of the genre, the story and approach makes it more approachable for first-time players, while providing what fans want to see.

How you present mechanics and systems is what defines the aesthetics of your game. With automation design, the king of the genre is still *Factorio* (released in 2016 by Wube Software), and the game does not try at all to create a cozy, or even casual, atmosphere – you are alone on a planet with monsters, and you must do everything you can to build up and survive. The automation and factory mechanics are highly advanced and open-ended, on top of setting up the needed defenses against enemies. With *Little Rocket Lab*, you are in a friendly town full of interesting people who want to see you succeed, with no monsters waiting to attack you.

I always provide this piece of advice with every *Deep Dive* I've written – do not pigeonhole yourself or your game's mechanics just because another game did it first. Every single indie game success story is always about trying to do something different; if they just repeated another game line-by-line, no one would be talking about it. A simple tweak can be all you need to create something original, and the market today is more receptive toward it (Figure 5.18).

Even more so with cozy/wholesome being thematic and not tied to specific mechanics. As a bit of a challenge, try to take something that normally would be in a high-stakes or violent game and make it cozy, and then see if you can do the opposite. Who knows, maybe you'll be the first to create the first cozy game about realistic sword fighting, or the first violent game built around hopscotch.

Figure 5.18

To end this chapter, I want to briefly talk about two of the most talked about RPGs released in 2024 and 2025 respectively between *Metaphor: ReFantazio* (developed by Atlus) and *Clair Obscur: Expedition 33*. Both games are by-the-book examples of Japanese role-playing games (JRPGs). However, both feature subtle and not so subtle differences with their aesthetics and gameplay to make them stand out from everyone else on the market that I don't have the space here to explore. Part of studying game design, and a goal of the Deep Dive series, is trying to get you to understand what aspects of a genre are foundational, and what you can manipulate to create something either brand new, or a different take on something everyone already knows.

6 A Cozy Conclusion

6.1 A Market Worth Exploring

Discussing cozy and wholesome games in this book has made me think about how much the market for video games has changed in the past 25 years. There was a time when designers predominantly catered toward hardcore gamers in the late 1990s and early 2000s, to the growing casual market of the late 2000s. Today, there are people celebrating hardcore experiences like *Elden Ring* just as there is an audience looking for a relaxing time (Figure 6.1).

Growing up from the 1980s to today, I've seen how much the definition of a video game has grown and so has the number of people who are interested in playing. For the first time, we are in a period where people who played and enjoyed video games as children are playing them as adults. Moreso, there are adults discovering the joy of games now; whether they are playing low- or high-stakes games.

Video games are no longer considered just a toy for children and something to grow out of; they can tell emotionally gripping stories, challenge someone with extreme situations, or just be something to unwind after a hard day's work. While there have been many studies over the years about how games improve cognition and hand-eye coordination, there are other studies on how games can help with

DOI: 10.1201/9781003646860-6

Figure 6.1

The game industry has come a very long way in 30 years. We've gone from focusing only on mechanics and gameplay, to becoming very serious about our games, and then getting very silly again. People can enjoy brutally difficult titles that push their skills to their limits or relax to a simple game about literally any subject. Just as there is no such thing as the perfect game, there is no perfectly defined consumer base. And while that may be scary for analysts and executives, for the reader, you live in a period where you are free to create what you want on any subject, and we'll never know what will be the next game concept to blow up.

emotional issues, depression, and provide people with an outlet for something they're dealing with.

And for the reader, you are free to develop whatever you want and tell a story that you feel strongly about. Each year, people are discovering that there is more to games than just the AAA releases, and we continue to see amazing games from the indie space reaching the mainstream.

Regarding the market for cozy games, I think Matthew said it best:

> Many people see wholesome games as a sudden response to an increasingly unstable, violent world. But if you talk to players, you'll quickly learn that many of us have always enjoyed these kinds of experiences and wanted more. Only recently, with the rise of indie games, have those players truly been catered to. And slowly but surely, larger studios and publishers are starting to take note.

Every year, the market for games has changed, with more variety happening. The old excuses of "genre X is not popular enough," which led to AAA studios only focusing on a few genres, have passed us. If a game is budgeted and scoped properly, it is possible to make even the smallest games work, but sustainability is a greater conversation the industry needs to have in the back half of the 2020s.

While writing this book between 2025 and 2026, studios and developers continue to face closures. Unions are starting to form among many of the larger companies, and we may at some point formally have a game dev union. There is no guarantee that the Game Industry as it exists now is going to be the same one by the end of the 2020's.

If we want to see amazing games, then people need to be free to create what they want. And with more people discovering games outside of the major studio releases, it means that there is now room to explore different kinds of games than there ever was before.

6.2 Will Cozy Change?

Like with every genre that has its breakout period, we are no longer in a period where cozy/wholesome games are considered new, and that begs the question: Will we see any design changes to the cozy/wholesome genres?

Our only point of reference in this respect would be the evolution of horror, which again is another thematic genre. Developers will always chase after whatever style is the biggest now, which leads to these cycles where a specific gameplay becomes the focus – such as social deduction games like *Among Us* (released in 2018 by Innersloth), *Balatro*, and as I mentioned earlier, with the entire farming sim trend courtesy of *Stardew Valley*. Even though most of the follow-up games to their respective hits did not succeed as well, this showed that there was more to explore within those designs rather than just making a direct copy.

Cozy and wholesome do have one advantage over horror when it comes to aesthetics – horror can fit in many different genres and stories, but its intent is always the same: to scare someone.

With cozy and wholesome games, everyone has their own opinions on what they want to see and the stories they want to tell (Figure 6.2). This creates a space where there are games that are about anything from running a store, coming to terms with death, starting a family, painting a house, and an infinite number of other activities.

As long as developers are inspired by their lives, there will be more cozy and wholesome games to come. With the previous comment from Matthew about how these games took off from the indie space, it made me think about why there haven't been more cozy games from AAA studios as of writing this in 2025. This is not a genre where you can just copy the story of another game and call it a day. The personal touch from these creators is a part of the appeal; something that is far harder to see in a 5–7-year AAA game developed by hundreds of people with different studios across the globe.

From a mechanical perspective, the main takeaway I want to see is more games that look at the model of *Stardew Valley* – present something that is easy to follow and to start playing and then grow that gameplay rather than just repeating the loop the same way. Story-focused games will always be around, but I do hope that

Figure 6.2

Sadly, not every inspiration for a video game can be a happy one, such as *That Dragon, Cancer* (released in 2016 by Numinous Games), which explored a family coming to terms with their four-year-old son dying of cancer – another example of how important it is to have a varied market for games that can explore many different topics.

we see people move away from saying that just because a game is cozy or wholesome, that it also must be incredibly simple.

I am also curious to see if virtual reality (VR) will have any impact on cozy games. Given that people have used VR for therapy sessions, I'm sure the space could be explored more with other ideas for cozy/wholesome games.

6.3 A Stress-Free Ending

This has been by far one of the hardest subjects to cover in the series, having to take a step away from design analysis to discuss one of the newest genres out there. The fact that the market in just about 6 years from when Wholesome Direct began is healthy enough to write a book discussing this form of design shows how much things have changed with people wanting more low-stakes games and why it grew so fast. The era when you could confidently say that people only want to play games of a certain type or a certain way is over. There are gamers who enjoy coming home from work to play some *Stardew Valley* and relax, just as there are people happy to start a new game of *Elden Ring* or play the latest horror game (Figure 6.3).

I said that the people who grew up playing games, including myself, are now adults, and we no longer live in a world that treats games and game design as nothing more than a fad. I've spoken to doctors, librarians, teachers, and even angel investors, who can talk to me about the favorite games they play today. It doesn't

Figure 6.3

Thank you for reading this *Deep Dive* all the way to the end. Just remember, everyone deserves some time to relax…or to rip and tear until it is done.

matter whether they come home and load up a *Minecraft* server, have a match of *Call of Duty*, or just tend to their farm in *Stardew Valley*, we all have our favorite ways of playing games.

The 2020s up until now have not been a pleasant decade, and I can't even begin to predict where the world will be by 2030, but I do know that people need a way to experience hope, even if it's as simple as building virtual dioramas or remembering to water their digital plants.

Glossary

Aesthetic: The mood or feeling a developer is trying to convey with the graphics and gameplay of their game.

DLC: Stands for "downloadable content" and is content for a game sold separately from the original purchase and can include everything from cosmetics to new gameplay and stories.

GUI: Stands for "graphical user interface" and covers all on-screen elements and windows the player will be viewing while playing a game.

Mechanic: An action or verb that the player is performing in the game.

Roguelike: A genre that focuses on restarting from scratch for each new game and challenges the player to adapt.

Soulslikes: A genre popularized by the *Dark Souls* series created by FromSoftware. Action-heavy games that focus on challenging fights and slower-paced combat.

System: A collection of mechanics that are connected to each other.

User experience: Used to describe how someone experiences a game's mechanics and to make that the best experience possible.

User interface: How someone directly interacts with a game through on-screen elements and the control peripheral.

UI/UX: Abbreviations for user interface and user experience.

Index

Pages in *italics* refer to figures.

For Product Safety Concerns and Information please contact our EU representative GPSR@taylorandfrancis.com
Taylor & Francis Verlag GmbH, Kaufingerstraße 24, 80331 München, Germany

www.ingramcontent.com/pod-product-compliance
Lightning Source LLC
LaVergne TN
LVHW010613110826
845149LV00003B/893

* 9 7 8 1 0 4 1 0 8 7 7 6 2 *